HIDING JESUS
THROUGH THE AGES

A Historical Study by
STEPHEN GRUBER, PH.D.

**Did first century rabbis conceal
the true messianic nature of Jesus
from the Jewish people?**

Hiding Jesus
Through the Ages

Note for Librarians: A cataloguing record for this book is available from Library and Archives Canada at www.collectionscanada.ca/amicus/index-e.html
ISBN 1-4120-5689-6

TRAFFORD

Offices in Canada, USA, Ireland and UK

This book was published *on-demand* in cooperation with Trafford Publishing. On-demand publishing is a unique process and service of making a book available for retail sale to the public taking advantage of on-demand manufacturing and Internet marketing. On-demand publishing includes promotions, retail sales, manufacturing, order fulfilment, accounting and collecting royalties on behalf of the author.

Book sales for North America and international:
Trafford Publishing, 6E–2333 Government St.,
Victoria, BC v8t 4p4 CANADA
phone 250 383 6864 (toll-free 1 888 232 4444)
fax 250 383 6804; email to orders@trafford.com
Book sales in Europe:
Trafford Publishing (uk) Ltd., Enterprise House, Wistaston Road Business Centre,
Wistaston Road, Crewe, Cheshire cw2 7rp UNITED KINGDOM
phone 01270 251 396 (local rate 0845 230 9601)
facsimile 01270 254 983; orders.uk@trafford.com
Order online at:
trafford.com/05-0587

10 9 8 7 6 5 4 3 2

To my beloved wife
Marilyn Kay Gruber
1951 – 2003

"It's the truth I'm after, and the truth never harmed anyone. What harms us is to persist in self-deceit and ignorance."

Marcus Aurelius
Second Century Roman Emperor
and philosopher: *Meditations*, 6:21

"Our truth nowadays is not what is, but what others can be convinced of."

Michel de Montaigne
16th Century French philosopher:
"Of giving the lie":
The Complete Essays

Contents

Acknowledgements

I would like to thank internationally recognized Judaic scholar Dr. Jacob Neusner for his kind help in directing me to excellent primary and secondary sources for this study. I have made use of many of his reference works which were immensely helpful as background source material. Thanks also to Dr. Ray McMurtry of Azusa Pacific University, for his helpful input and inspiration; to Dr. Edward N. Martin of Liberty University for reminding me that research should always produce more questions than answers; to Dr. Michael Andolina of Excelsior College for challenging me to consider wider perspectives, and to my editor, Mrs. Claudia Pendergrass, for her many helpful manuscript suggestions and clarifications. I am indeed indebted to these fine individuals.

Stephen Gruber
January 2005

Preface

I WAS FIRST DRAWN to the Messianic Christian movement while as a student in Chicago in 1972. At that time, Christian congregations that were made up of Jewish people who worshipped Jesus as the Messiah were generally known as "Hebrew Christian," or "Messianic Christian," and individual believing Jews were known as "Messianic Jews." These congregations were usually small, and their rabbis were sometimes Gentile.

In the ensuing decades, the Messianic Christian movement has grown significantly all over the world, with congregations in Israel including nations of the former Soviet Union and Russia.

The theological foundation of most Messianic congregations continues to be Evangelical in general, with many groups leaning toward the Pentecostal stripe with an emphasis on subjectivism and personal experience. Here one must be careful, because this does not reflect the theological roots of all adherents, but it would be fair, in my view, to suggest that it is for many. Thus, with a foundation of subjectivism and experience or "enthusiasm" in any group or movement, there is often a tendency to regard subjective "revelation" and knowledge as more important or relevant than objective study, or scholarship.

In my view, the Messianic movement over the past thirty years has lacked a substantive corpus of theological output. Like some sister groups within Evangelicalism, the Messianic movement has borrowed heavily from writers of other denominational structures in order to define their core doctrinal belief system. For example, popular Bible prophecy writer Hal Lindsey has borrowed heavily from earlier Evangelical writers such as C.I. Schofield and J. Darby to formulate his theory of End-Time prophecy, not-to-mention the current newspaper headlines that feature the Arab-Israeli crisis and oil in the Middle East. The Messianic movement has also adapted similar Evangelical views of the End-Times as pertaining to Israel and the coming of Messiah. When doctrinal statements of Messianic congregations are compared to various mainline Evangelical groups, there is often little difference, except in the use of Hebrew with English translations.

Perhaps one disadvantage of the lack of substantive scholarship within at least parts of the Messianic movement is that when new paradigms or hypotheses are born, there is often little existing research within the movement by which to measure accuracy. With regard to some within the Messianic movement, there is often a suspicion directed towards any scholar who is a "non-Christian," which, unfortunately, makes any objective discussion of a given topic virtually impossible.

One issue that has come to view within some circles in recent years, is that early rabbis at Yavneh, Palestine, around 70-80 CE, sought to hide the true identity of Jesus of Nazareth as Israel's true Messiah from the Jewish people. It is said that at Yavneh, Rabban (title for "my lord") Yohanan ben Zakkai, and other leaders, sought a policy of concealment, and actually wrote a "cursing" that was directed to the "minim," or writings of the heretics. This theory has been proposed by Hal Lindsey, *et al.*, and, if indeed true, certainly raises questions.

I have organized this volume into five chapters that may resemble any thesis or dissertation format. The reason why I have organized the material in this manner is so that the reader may follow my own journey from research question and sub-questions, to the method of research, the major body of relevant literature, my own presentation and analysis of the research, followed by my own conclusions and recommendations.

It is my hope that this presentation may provoke more questions and more research in the field. This study is not at all complete; the endnotes are designed to encourage further study in many areas that are only touched upon in this study. The bibliography, albeit selected, is also designed to aid the serious student. Quite frankly, in some ways, this book is not a fair and balanced historical presentation. There is no such a breed as a completely independent, fair and impartial, historian. However, my own journey in this project has been humbling; the beginning of wisdom for any sincere researcher/writer is to acknowledge personal prejudices and ignorance. Early on, I discovered that the body of literature appeared to lean more heavily to one side of the argument over the other. Still, I hope that my research and analysis gives a fair hearing to all. It may be of some note that my own conclusions differ quite sharply from some others within my own faith-group. I hope that with Divine wisdom, the reader will discern between my personal opinion and the historical data presented. To that end, I must plead human fallibility with the hope that in time further discovery and research may yield more light on the subject.

1

Introduction

THE LIFE AND TEACHINGS of Jesus of Nazareth have had a necessary connection to both biblical Judaism, i.e., the Old Testament, and rabbinic Judaism.[1] The concepts of man, man's responsibility, moral and ethical rules of conduct, sin and repentance, suffering, death, eternity and Messiah all find historical roots in the Holy Scriptures (Old Testament), discussion and commentary in the Talmud (ca. 200 BC-200 CE), and fulfillment in the New Covenant.[2] Remarkably, while the body of rabbinical literature had already been developing in Israel for two hundred years, Jesus appealed to the authority of the *tenach*, not to existing rabbinical writings. He reminded his audience that while "...you have heard what has been said of old," his final appeal to authority was always the Holy Scriptures.[3]

It was this continual appeal to the *tenach*, and not to tradition, that antagonized both the Pharisees and Sadducees.[4] In addition, the appeal of Jesus to objective authority apart from rabbinical teachings deeply antagonized rabbinical leadership and became even more intense when Jesus appealed to Yahweh (God) as his "Father."[5]

After three years of public ministry, Jesus was perceived by Jewish leaders to be a threat to the temple [6]and by Roman authorities to be a threat to the security of the Empire.[7] On the occasion of the Olivet Discourse, Jesus described the pending destruction of Jerusalem in eschatological language that left no doubt that those events described by Jesus would be fulfilled within the lifetime of his audience.[8] Following the crucifixion of Jesus, tensions in the Roman Empire between non-believing Jews in Jesus and believing "Nazarenes" continued unabated until, because of open hostility, in 52 CE, Emperor Claudius issued an edict that expelled both sects of Jews from Jerusalem.[9] The epistles of Paul give evidence that the relationship between the early Jewish *ecclesia* and Christian "Judiazers," was growing more tenuous and strained.[10] Within the Roman Empire, from the time of Paul's ministry in the mid-60's to the destruction and fall of Jerusalem in 70 CE, both Jews who did not believe in Jesus, and Jews who believed in Jesus as Messiah, were persecuted by the Romans.[11]

In the years that preceded the fall of Jerusalem, believers in Jesus heeded the words of their Lord, and fled the city to the town of Pella.[12] Additionally, thousands of Jews and non-messianic Jewish leaders, who survived the destruction of Jerusalem, fled Jerusalem north to the city of Yavneh (Roman: Jamnia).[13]

The coastal town of Yavneh consisted of two parts, a port and an inland borough, a commercial center located in the richest part of the plain near Lud, Bene Braq, Gimzo, Emmaus, and Azotus to the South-southwest. Yavneh's population consisted of merchants and craftsmen, and following the Jewish War with Rome, a large general population of Jewish peasants converged on the city with nowhere else to settle. Fortunately, Yavneh's population had been spared from most wartime activities.

Judaic scholar Jacob Neusner observes that the city had been a center of loyalty during the latter part of the war, and the population "did not bear ill feelings toward the refugee-rabbis and disciples."[14] Due to the pleasant coastal climate, the sages and rabbis were able to teach outside while making their living through trade or crafts. The leading rabbi and central historical figure of the Yavnean community was Rabban Yohanan ben Zakkai. The Rabban was indeed a controversial individual at a point in time when first century Judaism was in crisis.

From Jerusalem to Yavneh

Historian Max Dimont observes that the Jews came close to winning the war against the Roman Goliath, that Rome was forced to use her full military weight under Titus to besiege and destroy Jerusalem in 70 CE. The Jewish sages were watching closely, and the *pax Romana* ("peace of Rome") throughout the entire Roman Empire was at stake, for a Roman defeat in a Jewish uprising would not only bring universal humiliation to the might of Rome, but would fuel other revolts.

The Romans were taken completely by surprise in the first year of the war. In Syria Roman General Cestus Gallus brought his legions to subdue the Jewish revolt, but was defeated and driven back. In 66 CE the Jewish Revolt came to a fever pitch, and Emperor Titus knew that he had to take decisive action. Titus's most able general was Vespasian, and to him Titus gave command of Rome's most able legions. After a year of bitter fighting, Vespasian put his Galilean armies under the command of Joseph ben Mattathias, also known as Jewish historian Flavius Josephus (38-100 CE).

Josephus was born into a wealthy Palestinian Jewish family with a priestly background. Having been educated in the finest schools in Rome, Josephus then returned to Judea to pursue a military career, quickly rising to supreme commander of the Roman forces in Galilee. When the Galilean forces were destroyed, Josephus was taken before Emperor Vespasian, and in time the two became friends. Vespasian gave Josephus permission to accompany the Roman forces during the siege of Jerusalem in order to write the history of Rome's conquest of the Jews. For his action, the Jews branded Josephus a traitor, however, his two works, *History of the Jewish War,* and *Antiquities of the Jews*, stand as the most important histories that deal with the two centuries from 100 BCE to 100 CE.

As the war moved into the third year, Vespasian began to gain ground against the Jews. By 68 CE, Judea was captured, but Jerusalem seemed impregnable. Time after time, Vespasian attacked the city, but the Jews effectively thwarted each attack. The general then drew plans to lay siege to Jerusalem, convinced that the interruption of supplies and ensuing starvation would force the Jews to surrender. From the Roman vantage, the inhabitants of Jerusalem were now in check and could not freely come and go, and it was a matter of time before their sprit would be broken.

However, while the year 68 CE was militarily insignificant, the Jewish spiritual life was taking an upward turn. During this time, a rabbi-philosopher emerged from among the people—Rabban Yohanan ben Zakkai. Yohannan was a Pharisee, a disciple of Hillel, and a member of the Peace Party. Like Josephus, the Rabban was totally convinced that a zealot uprising against the Romans would only lead to certain massacre and to the possible extinction of Judaism itself. Yohanan at once deserted the war effort, and similar to Josephus, he would personally encounter Vespasian. Yet while Josephus in the first century would be labeled a traitor to the Jews, Yohanan would be acclaimed a savior of Judaism.

Yohanan ben Zakkai could see the coming conflagration that would overwhelm Palestine and the Diaspora that would be imposed upon his people. What Yohanan feared the most was the unwillingness or inability of the Jewish leadership to lay a new foundation for Jewish learning and that the heavy yoke of Rome would both doom Judaism and Jewish civilization to extinction. Yohanan became absorbed with an idea of a Jewish academy devoted to scholarship and the preservation of Judaism. As a virtual prisoner in a besieged city, Yohanan began to plan his own escape in order to gain an audience with the Emperor himself.

With each passing day, thousands of Jewish civilians died through starvation or disease. Jewish Zealots who suspected anyone of being a member of the Peace Party, physically threw such unfortunates over the city walls to their death. While the Romans were fortifying their battlements within striking distance of the city walls, the Zealots were completely in control of what little life remained within the city.

Yohanan realized that in order to escape the city, he must first outwit the Zealots. His ruse may seem to mirror a scenario from a modern spy thriller. Yohanan took a few of his closest disciples into his complete confidence and revealed his plan to them. Following this, his disciples moved into the city streets, tore their clothes, and with mournful wailing announced that their great rabbi, Yohanan ben Zakkai, had died of the plague. The disciples then asked the Zealot leaders permission to immediately bury the esteemed rabbi outside the city gates (according to the Law), so that the pestilence would not contaminate others.

As Yohanan's disciples wore sackcloth and ashes to display their grief, they slowly but deliberately carried a sealed coffin outside the city to Vespasian's tent. The coffin was opened and out stood Yohanan who looked calmly into the eyes of the surprised Roman general. The two men stood for some time looking at one another. Vespasian knew that this Jewish patriarch did not escape the city in a coffin only to save his own life. As the general waited, Yohanan chose his words carefully and spoke. The rabbi explained that his agenda was twofold: First, he had a prophecy pertaining to the general's career. Second, Yohanan had a personal request of the general. Yohanan then proceeded to tell Vespasian that he would soon be emperor. Then, Yohanan inquired, if Vespasian would grant Yohanan ben Zakkai and his disciples permission to organize a school or academy of Jewish learning in a Palestinian town where the rabbis could live their lives in peace and at the same time study Jewish Scripture.

Vespasian at first was overwhelmed by Yohanan's prophecy that he would soon be emperor, and then was overtaken by the modesty of Yohanan's simple request. Vespasian did not know that Yohanan's "prophecy" was in reality a calculated guess, for all Roman emperors were once generals. In that same year, 68 CE, Nero committed suicide. Following Nero's death, three political ruffians succeeded the throne, each assassinated after only a few months. In 69 CE, the Roman senate conferred the title

Emperor upon Vespasian who would now fulfill Yohanan's "prophecy." Vespasian then kept his promise to Yohanan who founded the first *yeshiva*, or Jewish academy
of learning, in the town of Yavneh.

This study will examine and re-evaluate the Yavnean
Academy and the activities of Yohanan ben Zakkai in
light of allegations of a deliberate "conspiracy" to cov-
er-up the identity of Jesus as Messiah from the Jewish
people.[15]

There is no single scholar more noted for his research
into the person of Yohanan ben Zakkai than renowned
Judaic historian Jacob Neusner.[16] Neusner presents a viv-
id portrait of Yohanan as a strong-willed, but determined
leader who reformulated community matters of law and
liturgy. Following the Jewish war with Rome from 66 to
70 CE, though he was a direct disciple of Hillel, Yohanan
ben Zakkai gave audience to various "Judaisms," including the new Nazarene movement, as providing interpretation of Judaism in first century crisis. The gathering of
rabbis at Yavneh was indeed an "academy" and not a religious "synod" or "council", having been started by Yohanan in about 80 CE. The academy was a direct result of
the Jewish War, and the various factions gathered there
to consider the current state and essence of Judaism with
a view to both develop and perpetuate Judaism within
Israel's community of faith "for all time."[17] Thus, I hope
to reevaluate the Academy at Yavneh and consider the
historical climate of that time that motivated the sages
there.[18]

Some Further Issues

In my view, anti-Semitism in attitude, word and action has reared its head during the history of the Christian church nearly from its inception. The Inquisition in
Spain is only one of hundreds of examples where Jews
were *carte blanch* denied civil and property rights by the
"church."[19] Tragically, as a whole, the Jewish people —
from the fall of Jerusalem in the first century to the Holocaust of the twentieth century — have suffered intense

persecution from Islamic incursions and wars, along with some quarters of organized Christianity. However, many historical examples abound where Christians have stood with their Jewish neighbors in defense of their human rights. [20]

Anti-Semitism by the Crusaders 900 years ago in Jerusalem was publicly acknowledged only recently in a "walk of reconciliation" by 2500 Christians who retraced the massacre trail of the Crusaders from Cologne, Germany, through Turkey, Syria, and Lebanon, "turning it into a repentance route." In April, 1999, the first teams entered Israel.[21] Organizer and Middle East Director, Matthew Hand, personally presented a letter of apology to Rabbi Lau in Jerusalem. [22]

Hopeful signs of reconciliation between religious groups are taking place in the world today, often initiated by Christians and others of good will. Oddly, however, there seems to exist a form of anti-Semitism within parts of Messianic Judaism that is directed towards non-Christian Jewish leaders. The term, "Messianic Judaism," designates a group of Jewish people who have come to believe that Jesus is the Messiah, but for cultural reasons, desire to maintain Jewish identity in worship liturgy, manners, and customs. The term may also apply to Gentile believers who identify with the "Jewishness" of their faith and are comfortable with expressing their faith in a totally Jewish cultural and liturgical context.

Over the course of many years, Messianic Judaism has taken on different forms and expressions. While I identify with the "Jewishness" of my faith as embodied in both the Old and New Testaments, I have also seen some theological leanings that are out of the mainstream of accepted and known research. For example, the historically undocumented claim by some that the original autographs of the New Testament were not written in Greek, but rather in Hebrew, and that the original Hebrew autographs were deliberately destroyed by the early church.

As a result, some leaders of the Messianic Movement in the United States, ironically, appear to harbor an attitude toward all non-Messianic Jewish leadership which has characteristics of anti-Semitism. For example, Phillip Moore's 1996 book titled, *The End of History – Messiah Conspiracy*, though while claiming a pro-Israel stand, has many vitriolic passages that target religious Jewish leaders in general. [23] Moore has served as researcher for popular writer Hal Lindsey, as the book claims, and alleges that recent "evidence" has come to light that categorically proves that a "conspiracy" took place at Yavneh to conceal the true identity of Jesus of Nazareth from the Jewish people in Israel.[24] But is there solid historical evidence to support such a claim?

The historical problem centers on the nature and scope of the Yavnean Academy, ca. 70-135 CE. If it is true, as Jacob Neusner and others have written, that the Academy at Yavneh reformulated Judaism in the wake of the Jewish War, then two basic branches of Judaism emerged. First, one branch of Judaism descended from Hillel that was reformulated through the strong leadership of Yohanan ben Zakkai. The second was the Judaism of Jesus of Nazareth that was promulgated by Peter (to the Jews) and Paul (to the Gentiles).

Dr. Neusner agrees that the *menim* malediction recorded in the Talmud may have been directed toward Jewish believers in Jesus, however that there is no historical evidence of a "conspiracy" to conceal Jesus' true identity as Israel's Messiah, a theory that will be examined in detail.[25]

Under the chapter heading, "Twenty Centuries of Deception," Philip Moore writes "For nearly twenty centuries, rabbis of all branches of contemporary Judaism, which was reconstructed at Yavneh, have been successful in convincing nine-tenths of world Jewry that Jesus is not for the Jews and that He is not worthy of Messianic consideration." [26] Thus, the world's Jewish community "have been the victims of a conspiracy perpetrated upon them by a small group of elitist rabbis who gathered at Yavne [sic] nearly 2000 years ago." [27]

Judaic scholars James Parkes, Jakob Jocz, *et al.*, seem to agree. Popular writer Hal Lindsey mirrors a similar conclusion: "In Yavne [sic)] they hammered out the basis of rabbinic [sic] Judaism... to isolate and insulate the Jewish person completely from Jesus — completely."[28]

However, Judaic scholar Jacob Neusner departs from this hypothesis. Neusner's voluminous writings span over thirty years, and he concludes that Yohanan ben Zakkai's activity at Yavneh, from about 70 to 85 CE, was mostly legal and liturgical in nature. The various "Judaisms" of the day, including the more recent Nazarene sect, were given audience and consideration by the sages. [29]

The divergence of the two branches of Judaism appears to have been gradual, beginning first with the Gospel teachings of Jesus in contrast to the teachings of the Scribes and Pharisees, and continuing with the Pauline formulation that conflicted with the "Judaizers" that culminated at Yavneh about a decade after the Jewish War. Messianic expectations by Messianic (Christian) Jews were abundantly different from their non-Messianic Jewish counterparts who viewed Christianity as an aberrant movement *within* first century Judaism.

The historical question naturally evolves from the current debate within the Messianic movement in the United States: before 1925, scholars in the field of Judaic studies believed that the *minim* mentioned in the Mishnah were heretics in general; the reformulation of the "Eighteen" Benedictions (*ve-lamalshinim*) was specifically designed to exclude them from Israel and the synagogue.

Israeli scholar Gedaliah Alon (1980) observes that, in 1925, the question appeared to be settled with the discovery of the Cairo Genizah fragments that contained portions of the liturgy according to ancient Palestinian rite.[30] Some within the Messianic community in the United States have interpreted this discovery as a deliberate concealment of the identity of Jesus the Messiah from the Jewish masses.

Other scholars, such as Conzelmann, Cohen, Wilson, Setzer, Notet and Kimmelmann, assert that the historical sources are unclear regarding *the birkat ha-Minim*, which is the primary foundation for the alleged concealment theory. Current scholars, such as Cohen and Neusner, interpret the historical accounts, primarily from the Mishnah, as affirming that Messianic Christianity of the first century was deemed a legitimate branch of Judaism until late in the second or early third century.

As we take a closer look at the historical evidence, other questions are important to keep in mind:

- What was the origin of the Yavneh Academy?
- What was Rabban Yohanan ben Zakkai's position at Yavneh?
- What other sects were present at Yavneh?
- What were some of the theological challenges to Yohanan?
- What impact did Rabban Hillel have on Yohanan?
- How was authority transferred from the Jerusalem council to Yavneh?
- What were Yohanan's public policies at Yavneh?
- What did Yohanan achieve at Yavneh?
- What was the nature of the opposition to those policies?
- What relationship existed between Vespasian and Yohanan that led to the founding of the academy at Yavneh?
- Who was the *minim* spoken about in the Mishnah?
- What motivated the Yavnean Sages to exclude *carte blanche* Jewish Christians from their ethnic identity?
- What was the true nature of the "parting" between traditional rabbinical Judaism and Christianity?

The reader should be aware that it is possible that initial questions may defy a clear answer, while at the same time other questions may surface.

Unfortunately, we are limited to few existing primary, with a wide scope of interpretation by scholars on all sides of the issues. In a real sense, this study is provided in summary form, with detailed citations, and a selected bibliography. The researcher is often limited to the interpretation of the data in the rabbinic sources, for at times source material is unclear or contradictory. For example, the Tradition (Mishnah) records three versions of Yohanani's escape from Jerusalem and subsequent meeting with General Vespasian. Additionally, it is unclear from the primary source whether Yohanan ben Zakkai actually pleaded to be sent to Yavneh with his disciples, or if the Romans, fearing another uprising by the Jews, compelled Yohanan and his followers against their will to be detained at Yavneh.

Thus, the research is often limited to variant accounts, brief passages, unclear expression of activity, or as in the case with the Mishnah, uncertainty in chronological order of events. We are often unsure if certain policies were actually implemented during the time of Yohanan, or came much later during the time of Gamaliel II.[31]

2

An Overview of Key Historical Sources

Part One: Yavneh and Yohanan ben Zakkai, ca. 80 CE

IT IS IMPOSSIBLE to review, analyze and summarize all of the research that pertains to the issue at hand. Relevant scholarly and academically credible sources that pertain to Yavneh will be presented and discussed in this chapter with in-paragraph citations for quick reference. Detailed footnotes in later chapters and a bibliography are provided to aid in further research. Grabbe (1992) insists that much of the reconstruction of Yavneh by older scholarship must be discarded or extensively revised.

Although the Jewish historian Josephus never mentioned Yohanan ben Zakkai by name, in Mishnah tradition the philosopher-rabbi had received permission to form an academy of learning in the town of Yavneh (Roman: Jamnia) by the Emperor Vespasian (Saldarini, 1975; Neusner; 1969, 1980). The historical incident is regarded as fundamentally important in Jewish history, despite the fact that most of our knowledge is derived from Jewish literature. We know less of the actual details, except by interpretative historical accounts of older secondary studies. Events may even have gone unnoticed by many Jews at the time (Grabbe, 1992).

The main problem, notes Stemberger (1995), in the investigation Yavneh is that the early rabbinic texts barely document the rabbinic heritage; in fact, they appear rather to conceal it. This makes the investigation of a continuum bridging the year 70 CE especially difficult. The Mishnah plays a special role as the basic document of rabbinic Judaism.

Yohanan ben Zakkai, founder of the school at Yavneh, was never designated a "Pharisee" (*m.Yad*. 4.6). Only later was he was succeeded by Rabban Gamaliel II, whom the Mishnah designates a Pharisee, but this narrative of the replacement of Gamaliel by the high priest Eleazar ben Azariah is probably to be interpreted as a reference to leadership struggles in the new movement (Stemberger, 1995). In any event, the literature strongly suggests that the Yavnean leadership occupied a tenuous and specious position at Yavneh, suggesting that the peasantry viewed with suspicion the rabbis' authority (Jocz, 1948; Alon, 1980). Thus, a "conspiracy" to conceal Jesus — his true identity — from the people would have been highly improbable, if not impossible, considering the many references to both his ministry and person in secular literature (see Chapter Four).

Ben-Sasson (1969) argues that according to earlier Palestinian traditions, Rabban Yohanan ben Zakkai was initially a prisoner of general Vespasian, taken against his will to Yavneh, which, along with other towns, such as Ashdon and Gophna, served as a place of detention for those who had surrendered to the Romans. Cohen (1989), Neusner (1976) *et al.*, suggest that the historical sources are too obscure and any theory is pure speculation.

This position was taken by in the last two decades by Jacob Neusner and his team of researchers, of the Mishnah and Tosefta (Neusner: *A History of the Mishnaic Law*, 1974-77; 1980b; 1981-83; 1983-85). A large portion of the recent evidence and analysis is provided in Neusner's, *Judaism: The Evidence of the Mishna*, and prosopographic rabbinic literary traditions.

The Jewish town of Yavneh had become a Roman possession; to the Jews Vespasian's concession to Yohanan gave particular significance to Yavneh. The Romans sanctioned — or at least tolerated — the Yavneh academy in which first century Judaism would be reconstructed (Schurer, 1885; Neusner, 1980). Though Yavneh is referenced in some literature as a "synod," it was not a church council, but an academic enterprise devoted to Judaic scribes of Torah and sages. At first, the number of participants was few, and the members were not regarded as representative of all Jews in Palestine. The Yavnean Pharisees who influenced the Mishnah's final form also influenced Jewish society (Alon, 1980; Dunn, 1992).

Excellent source material is available in the rabbinic tradition (Goodblatt, 1980), however, narrative history or biography is impossible due to the nature of the extant sources (Neusner, 1980; Green 1978, 1980). Analysis of the sources demonstrates a development of religious ideas in the major stages of Mishnah growth (Neusner, 1980; 1981). Prior to the fall of Jerusalem in 70 CE, the four areas of most interest in Judaism were agriculture, festivals, purity, and women.

A closer investigation of the academy at Yavneh indicates that the Old Testament was not canonized there (Grabbe, 1992). Shaye J.D. Cohen (1987) and Jakob Jocz (1948) disagree. Cohen observes that until recently, scholars understood the rabbinic "synod" at Yavneh as having finalized the canonization of the Hebrew Bible around 100 CE, but this view has lost support, "primarily because of lack of evidence." These scholars, Cohen urges, also assumed that the Yavnean rabbis were motivated by a desire to exclude Christianity from the fold and to exclude Christian and apocalyptic books from the canon. They insist that this interpretation has no historical substance (1987).

The overwhelming majority of the literature agrees that it cannot be demonstrated historically that the Yavnean Pharisees administered society in either the civil or religious arena; rather, Yavneh represents in Jewish history merely a transitional period that would lead to rabbinic dominance of Jewish life.

Yavnean Judaism owed a great debt to the tradition of pre-70 CE Judaism (Cohen, 1984). Yohanan provided a synthesis of traditions, and there is little evidence that he was a traditional Pharisee (Neusner, 1979: 30-32, 36-37). On the contrary, Yohanan provides all the characteristics of a Pharisee who saw his religion based on Scripture. It was probably Yohanan—in light of this important distinction in Judaism—who gave vision to the reconstruction and reorientation at Yavneh and who outlived the destruction of the temple by little more than a decade (Grabbe, 1992). Yohanan spoke of Torah-study as the goal of human life (Neusner, 1976; 1994).

Yohanan speaks of the study of the Torah as the very purpose for which the human being was created. The question in the academy of *Lod,* "Study or practice?" was soundly answered at Yavneh with the emphasis on practice, but in no way intended to deprive study of the Torah's primacy (Kaplan, 1934).

George Foot Moore (1927) observes that for Yohanan, study, as well as prayer, is true worship, and is effectual by means of the service of the altar. Moore argues—quoting *Berakot* 5b (Mishnah), that the rabbis at Yavneh, compared their scholarly work to that of the peasants in the fields, for "humility is the condition of true learning."

The Yavnean academy became the "high court" capable of issuing authoritative enactments. Yohanan's method was that of Hillel, Gamaliel I, and Simeon ben Gamaliel before him to issue decrees on specific legal problems (Neusner, 1975). Through Yohanan's leadership, the interpretation of the Law was carried on with great zeal in the wake of the political overthrow by the Romans. Everything pertaining to it, for example, the criminal and the civil law and the manifold religious statutes and ordinances, were dealt with by these scholars with painful observance, and "drilled into the memories of the scholars by their teachers" (Schurer, 1890). His ordinances met some opposition, mainly from the priests, but in time they were accepted.

Yohanan's main task was to persuade the Jews to admit into the synagogue some of the ceremonies of the temple other than the sacrifices. This would make the synagogue the heir to the temple (Grayzel, 1947). When the Yohanan died (ca. 85 CE), the tradition says that his generation recited concerning him (quoting Song of Solomon 8:7), "If a man should give all the wealth of his

house for the love" with which R. Yohanan loved the Torah, "he would be utterly destitute" (Mishna).

In pre-70 Pharisaism, the major concern was with religious law. The dominant schools of Pharisees at Yavneh
were those of Hillel and Shammai (Charlesworth and
Johns, 1997). Each of these schools, and the other sects
present at Yavneh, had their own individual rulings that
differed from one another, and represented the interests of Pharisees whose spheres of authority were their
homes and sects.

At Yavneh these differences were debated profusely
(Neusner, 1969;1980). We can only speculate at the political drama that existed in the Yavnean community, but
eventually the school of Hillel dominated the discussions, and later the reformulation of first century Judaism (Grabbe, 1992).

The opening of the school at Yavneh was not the only
contribution of Yohanan to the restoration of Judaism.
There was an urgent need of a body competent to determine matters of grave importance to all Jews; foremost
was the fixing of the calendar thereby amending the cor-
rect dates of all the festivals and feasts (Moore, 1927). In
addition, many questions arose from the cessation of the
temple worship, without precedent, and an authoritative
decision was necessary to end the confusion of the practice. Therefore, the focus of the Yavnean academy was
not merely the consideration of all the other "sects" of
Judaism and a *minim* pronouncement — nor was its impetus to conceal information — but the doctors of the Law
at Yavneh considered liturgical and legal matters urgent
for all Jews.

Part Two: The Mishnah (ca. 200 BCE — 200 CE)

When the Babylonians destroyed the Temple in 586
BCE, Israelite sages began writing their history to both
record and interpret what had actually happened [the
fall of Jerusalem and the destruction of the temple in 70
CE would cause the Yavnean rabbis to query "why" the
temple was *again* destroyed] (Neusner, Green and Fr-

erichs, 1987). When the temple fell to the Romans, established patterns of thinking guided Jewish apocalyptic writers to consider the meaning of Israel's history. In the view of the Gospel writers, Jesus was Israel's Messiah, *the* Messiah at the end of time, Savior, Redeemer of Israel from historical calamity, historical-political figure: *King of the Jews*.

The character of the Israelite Scriptures emphasized historical narrative as a mode of theological explanation, thus Judaism evolved as a Messianic religion. Actions are prescriptive to the coming of Messiah at the end of time, and rabbinic interest focused upon answering the question—"How long?"

The Mishnah represents a vast and influential document presenting a kind of Judaism within the context of a non-historical system. The Mishnah presents a systematic account of the life of Israel in the land of Israel, a composition of sixty-three tractates covering six categories of activity including conduct of the economy, farmers' provision and priestly rations. In addition, there are rules concerning holy days, seasons, and sacrificial conduct.

Then there are rules concerning the status of women, a code of civil laws covering all aspects of commercial, civil, and criminal law, and a governmental blueprint headed by a king or high priest in the temple of Jerusalem. While the framers of the Mishnah certainly had a theory of the Messiah, they kept it hidden (Neusner, Green and Frierichs, 1987).

The expression "rabbinic period" in the literature connotes the fact that we are well informed about the rabbis and about no one else. One of the remarkable characteristics of the Mishnah is how little information the text reveals about itself, its origins, authors, sources, history, and social setting (Cohen, 1987). The Yavnean period shows a transitional phase in the Mishnah as it moved into its final form. What is noted is little development of the *Neziqin* (civil law), which indicates that the Pharisees at Yavneh had no administrative influence in society as a whole.

The Mishnah was a philosophical law code brought to closure at about 200 CE and is not indicative of a Judaism framed in response to Christian pressures (Neusner, 1995). In particular, the document addressed issues pertinent to the destruction of the temple and the subsequent defeat to bring a monarchal restoration. Thus, the issues that gave definition to the Mishnah's historical context were twofold: First, the destruction of the temple in 70 CE, and second, the defeat of Bar Kokhba in 135 CE.

There is extensive discussion in creating a new, idealized Judaism, not in extending or developing the old second temple practices (Grabbe, 1992). In the wake of the destruction of the temple and Jerusalem in 70 CE, and the final defeat in 135 CE, Jewish sages developed a Judaism within a temple and a cult context. This produced the Mishnah in which a system of sanctification focused on the holiness of the priesthood, cultic festivals, the temple and its sacrifices, as well as on the rules for protecting holiness from levitical uncleanness (Neusner, 1995). Only later after Julian "the Apostate" did the sages work out a Judaic system of salvation that would focus on the salvific power of the sanctification of the holy people.

The system pictured in the Mishnah came forth in a world before the advent of Jesus of Nazareth. First, the Mishnah does not explicate a systematic theory of Scriptural authority, which gives explanation to the continual conflict between Jesus and the Pharisees in the Gospels (Neusner, 1995; Parks, 1960).

Second, a theory of the relationship of the oral to the written Torah. The sages did not undertake a systematic exegetical effort at the linking of the principal document, the Mishnah, to Scripture because there was no obvious need. Christianity pressed the question of the status of the Mishnah in relationship to Scripture, and claimed that the Mishnah was "man made" and not God's inspired will found only in the Scripture (Mark 4:4, etc.).

Third, there is no teleology focused on the coming of the Messiah as the end and purpose of the Mishnah system as a whole. Mishnah theology does not have an

eschatological context whatsoever; the lack of an eschatological focus necessarily precluded a coming Messiah.

Last, this same Judaism that formulated the Mishnah
provided little emphasis on the symbol of the Torah,
even though since the time of Moses there was a preeminence of Torah.

In retrospect as both the Mishnah and the Gospels are
considered in light of first century Judaism, the sages
produced a document so entirely independent of Scripture that the sages used their own words to suggest what
the Scriptures had declared (Neusner, 1995).

Part Three: Roman Occupation of Palestine;
Pre- and Post-War Conditions (ca. 70–135 CE)

As far as the Romans were concerned – at least during
the reign of Vespasian and Titus – the Jews were accorded
legal status throughout the empire that was not basically
altered by the violent Jewish War of 66-70 CE, despite the
structural changes that Judaism underwent as a result of
the loss of Jerusalem and the temple and provincial reorganization of Palestine (Conzelmann, 1992).

The legal and social status of the Jews was preserved
in Antioch and Alexandria (Josephus, *War*, 100ff; *Ant.*
12.120ff). The Jews in this period under the Flavians enjoyed a time of peace and tranquility, but Hegesippus
reported an incident (disputed in Jewish sources) of
persecution under Vespasian (Eusebius, *Hist. Eccl.* 3.12).
Smallwood (1976) writes that no evidence exists for a
Jewish uprising after 80 CE.

Both Christians and Jews reflected upon the destruction of Jerusalem and the "great sanctuary." They would
later look at the alleged misdeeds of those who lived at the
time for reasons to account for the destruction (Neusner,
1984). No generation in the history of Jewry had been
so roundly and universally condemned by posterity as
that of Yohanan ben Zakkai. Christians remembered the
words of their Lord in Matthew 23:37-39 in reference to
the city of Jerusalem "killing the prophets and stoning
those who are sent to (them)." And when the disciples

pointed out the temple buildings from a distance, Jesus commented that those very stones would not be left standing upon one another (Matt 24:2; cf. Luke 21:6).

On these passages, the Jews after the destruction of Jerusalem said no less: that because of their own sins they had been expelled from their own land (*War*, 1.18ff; 7.8.6; *Ant.*, 20:11.1)..

The rich and powerful — especially the high priests and important priestly families — controlled the temple and were its primary beneficiaries. Herod's expansion of the temple complex in 20 BCE, consolidated his power and increased his status. The indigenous Judean oligarchy was essentially nepotistic, and the temple system during the Herodian period was agrarian which continued with punishing taxation and provided little benefit to the peasantry (Hanson and Oakman, 1998). Thus, when Jesus rejected the temple as a "cave of bandits", he rejected it as a utilitarian institution of redistribution that benefited only a few and degraded many.

The Jesus movement that began with a concern for institutional reform was temporarily quenched with the crucifixion of its Founder. The destruction of Jerusalem — and the temple institution fueled by a corrupt Roman government and religious "puppet" authority — made any "reformation" irrelevant.

Life in Judea following the fall of Jerusalem is far less documented historically than the period prior to the fall. The historian Josephus reported on events that immediately followed the destruction in clear fashion; otherwise the student is left with incidental references from classical authors, a few extant Roman inscriptions, archaeological artifacts, coins, and rabbinic traditions (Hayes & Mandell, 1998).

The Jewish rebels still occupied countless caverns and caves when Titus left Judea accompanied by the vast majority of the Roman forces. Bassus was given the grim task of forcibly removing the rebels. Probably in late 71 CE, Herodium, Herod's burial place seven miles southeast of Jerusalem was taken with minor difficulty (*War* 7.163).

The Jewish stronghold Machaerus in the Transjordan was a severe obstacle to Roman domination. When the Romans began to construct a rampart across the 150-foot ravine, the rebels surrendered the fortress without a struggle in exchange for safe passage when one rebel was captured, flogged, and threatened with crucifixion (*War* 6.164-209). The rebels used the forest of Jardes as a refuge for those who escaped from Jerusalem and Machaerus, but in time the Romans surrounded and massacred three thousand rebels sustaining no casualties of their own (*War* 7, 210-15).

In the meantime, numbers of rebels fled Judea for Alexandria and Cyrene. In Alexandria their presence led to intramural fighting in the Jewish community followed by Roman mass executions (*War* 7.409-19). The Romans — desiring to send a strong message to the rebels — destroyed the Jewish temple of Onias IV that was built at Leontopolis in Egypt (Cf. *Ant.* 13.70; *War* 7.420-36). With Jerusalem in ruins, Machaerus captured, the Christian Jews in Pella and thousands of refugees and rabbis in Yavneh, Masada alone remained to be taken. Flavius Silva succeeded Bassus who died in Judea, and took his post in late 72 or early 73 CE. A year later the last Jewish stronghold of Masada was taken by the Romans (*War.* 2.447; 7.253; 275-79; 6.280-84, 304-19). Roman domination during the Yavnean period brought many changes in Judean life, some economical and others political. The inhabitants of Palestine became impoverished, and by the Seven Years' War (1756-63) their numbers had been terribly reduced.

The Jewish people maintained an indomitable hope that one day, under an established civil government, even among the nations of the world, they "would come again to have a recognized place and practical authority" (Schurer, 1885). Despite the lack of information that surrounds the historical events, we have enough information to reconstruct and appreciate the vitality of the Yavnean period in Jewish history. The Judaism of our time owes its roots to the sixty years following the destruction of Jerusalem wherein rabbinic Judaism was born (Grabbe, 1992).

Part Four: Judaism and Christianity:
The Emergence of Two Distinct Judaisms
(ca. 70–135CE)

Our knowledge of the history of Judaism in the post-70 CE period comes almost exclusively from rabbinical texts. Pagan, Christian, and archaeological sources contribute some detail, but little more (Cohen, 1987). Christianity arose from the matrix of Judaism and was a form of Judaism until the Christians were expelled from the synagogue around the end of the first century. The initial separation was not, however, due to theology. Rather, in Palestine Christians tended to disassociate themselves from the national movement, and pacifistic withdrawal from the revolt against Rome led to alienation from non-Christian Jews (Sigal, 1980).

Dunn (1992) identifies four pillars of Second Commonwealth Judaism: (1) monotheism (God is one), (2) election (Israel is chosen by God), (3) the covenant (affirmed by Torah), and (4) the Land (Jerusalem and the temple included). Dunn explores the various ways both Jews and Christians understood these pillars and discovers in their variant understandings the seeds of separation. In Dunn's view, Christians became increasingly critical of both the temple establishment and the temple itself. As Luke chronicled, a rising view was that the temple was viewed as constructed "with human hands" (Acts 7:48), with idolatrous implications. Early Christians believed that God no longer resided in the temple, but his tabernacle was within "the body of Christ." Jesus died once for all, and Christians would themselves be "a holy priesthood acting as ministers of reconciliation" (cf. 2 Cor 5:18; 1 Pet 2:5, 9; Rev 1:6; 5:10; 20:6).

In the view of the common Jewish peasant, that Jewish Christians would not defend Jerusalem from the onslaught of Rome caused many to question the authentic "Jewishness" of the Nazarene movement. In their view, no true Jew would abandon the temple to be desecrated by pagan gentiles (Cohen, 1987; Conzelmann, 1992).

In the early twentieth century, Jewish existential philosopher Martin Buber in his widely acclaimed examination of historic Judaism titled, *On Judaism* (1965), recognized the Judaic nature of the early church juxtaposed to the church of the twentieth century. Buber pronounces "original Judaism" on the early pre-Yavnean Nazarene movement, even "a movement more closely related to Judaism than to what is today called Christianity."

In the first century CE prior to the destruction of Jerusalem, various sects comprised "Judaism." These included Essenes, Pharisees, Sadducees, Qumran Jews, Zealots, Sicarri, Christian Jews, "the Fourth Philosophy," Samaritans, Therapeutae, and others (Cohen, 1987). Following the destruction, by contrast, Judaism was not marked by sectarianism, though Samaritans persisted in a marginal group in Jewish society and were active in their own right.

By the end of the first century, Christianity had already traveled far beyond Palestine through the vast regions of the Roman Empire, and became predominantly gentile – a separate religion from the historic Judaism of the sages. By the time of John Chrysostom in 423 CE, Christianity was almost exclusively a gentile religion, and Christian emperors legislated to restrain local Christians from attacking synagogues (cf. *CTh.* 16..8.9 393 CE; 16.8.2; Cameron, 1993), while all other groups virtually disappeared from view. Exceptions included a few rabbinic and patristic references to the second temple period (Cohen, 1987).

The increasing distance between Judaism and Christianity at the beginning of the second century meant that very few Jewish works written after 100 CE were incorporated in the literary heritage of the new religion. The fact that so little Jewish non-rabbinic literature exists from the Yavnean period would indicate that neither the rabbis nor the Christians desired to preserve this material; it does not necessarily proves that such literature never existed. Cohen believes that after 70 CE many

Jews—perhaps most Jews—did not yet regard the rabbis as their legitimate leaders, and did not regard rabbinic Judaism as the standard of behavior and belief (1987). If this is true, then how much more illogical to suppose that leaders who were already viewed with angst and skepticism could deliberately and successfully conceal the identity of Jesus as Messiah from their own people following a war that demolished virtually all internal sectarianism.

The rabbis at Yavneh had no desire to exclude anyone, let alone the Christians. Still, through three centuries, from the time of Jesus to Constantine, Christianity was unlike all pagan religions, for it more closely resembled Judaism (Neusner, 1995; Buber, 1960). In the first century, Christians considered their faith the Judaism predicted by the prophets and fulfilled in Yeshua the Messiah. Like their brethren in the flesh, Christian Jews read the Torah and claimed to perceive and declare its true meaning, and like Israel, claimed that they alone worshipped the one true God.

One point of conflict arose early when Christians—led by Paul—claimed to be the "true Israel," promulgators of the Israel of the promises and grace of ancient Scripture. The sages, whose leadership positions at Yavneh were at best dubious in the eyes of the people, could not have avoided the issue of the place, within the Torah's messianic pattern, of the remarkable turn in world history represented by the triumph of Christianity.

Another point of conflict, as Evans and Hagner (1993) and Gager (1995), have observed, is that some of the critiques in the Gospels contributed to a later polemic that drove Christians out of the synagogue and away from Judaism. They cite John 8:44 ("you are of your father the devil") as an example of language taken as vitriolic, or at best an angry exchange. But the authors are careful to maintain that the Gospel material, though forthright, was in its original composition an in-house debate and polemic, and not anti-Semitic. This polemic material, however, provided an increasingly gentile church with a major corpus of authoritative tradition from which anti-Semitic ideas were fostered in some church fathers.

The Judaism of the early twentieth century tradition-ally viewed Jesus as "one who was so preoccupied with the individual and his salvation that he has little to say about society," in contrast to a Judaism that speaks to society's needs (Steinberg, 1947). It is alleged that Jesus made no proposals about measures to abolish slavery, the rights of the free laborer and how they may be as-sured, about the all-devouring statism of the Roman Empire and how to oppose it (Sigal, 1980). It is widely regarded that the social gospel of Jesus is so slight that Christendom has had to reach behind him to the proph-ets of the Old Testament for its political and economic ideals (Steinberg, 1947; Hertzberg, 1961).

However, the Judaism of the late twentieth century, with the benefit of archaeological discovery, provides a more balanced view of Jesus as a Pharisee more tradi-tionally aligned with the school of Hillel, whose ethical teaching spoke of a heart transformation in relation to society, rather than strict obedience to the Law (Charles-worth, 1997).

Paul's development of an argument on the basis of Scripture in Galatians 4 is inextricably connected with his emphasis upon the activity of the Spirit within those who are baptized. It is vital to recognize that connection before Paul's arguments from Scripture can be under-stood (Neusner and Chilton, 1997).

Steinberg argues that Paul, in contrast to Jesus, was a product of the Greco-Roman world, and not traditional Judaism (Steinberg, 1961). Cohen argues that the reason for Paul's persecution by the "Judaizers" early in the new Christian movement was largely because of Paul's (and Jesus') teaching of "freedom from the Law and the libertine consequences which he and his followers drew from it" (Smith, 1996).

The view largely held by Jewish scholars today is that the cause of persecution of Christians by Jews, was not the preaching of the crucifixion, but the open teaching and practice of freedom from the Law (Smith, 1996, citing Gal 6:13). Steinberg (1961) and Hertzberg (1947) both emphasize the importance of the Law. Steinberg comments: "Law is an element in Judaism...because of the intense Jewish preoccupation with ethics, and because of the historic Jewish insistence that ideals need to...work" (145).

For the Law to become personal, argues Steinberg, there is an insistence in the Law that must be translated into habits and disciplines. "If they be social they must be incarnated in institutions, folkways, and law. Otherwise, their cogency and content will evaporate, and they will be left in the end empty vessels." Yet this translation of Law by Steinberg does not preclude the teachings of Jesus (e.g., Sermon on the Mount, Matthew 5) in which he lays heavy emphasis on a transformed heart in the tradition of Hillel (and Yohanan ben Zakkai) that leads to obedience.

Chilton and Neusner (1995) suggest that the context of all Judaism find its definition in the urgent question, "How does humanity come to know God?" Further, "What are the terms of God's entry into the world?" The answer is through God's self-manifestation to Israel. For traditional Judaism, they argue, this conception comes to expression in so many words: God entered the world on account of Israel, and God departed from the world because of Israel's actions.

At greater issue was the context of what constituted the true "Israel": the Israel according to the flesh, as Paul explained, or the Israel of the Spirit. Who or what is "Israel"? When we speak of Jesus Christ, we invoke a category that is no more "biographical" or historical than when we speak of Israel, where we invoke a category that is ethnic (Chilton and Neusner, 1995). In both cases, we find ourselves engaged in a profound inquiry into *how* God and humanity meet: Israel or Christ, Torah or Christ—both formulation serve, each its own Judaism, none of which are confluent.

The issue of *who* was "Israel" ultimately divided the early Christian church from rabbinical Judaism. By claiming that "Israel" constituted "Israel after the flesh," the actual family of Abraham, the sages met head-on the Christian claim that there was—or could ever be—some *other* "Israel," of a lineage not defined by the family connection at all, and that the existing Jews no longer constituted "Israel" (Neusner, 1995). Had this been the only issue at Yavneh, a split between the two Judaisms most certainly would have ensued.

Jews of the second century interpreted the phrase "synagogue of Satan" (Rev 3:8-9) as referring to non-believing Jews. Cohen argues that the author of Revelation believed that the title "Jew" (*Ioudaios*) was an honorable designation and properly belonged only to those who believed in Christ, just as Paul said that the real Jew was not one designated outwardly through circumcision but through circumcision of the heart and in the spirit (1999, citing Romans 2:28-29).

Christian appropriation of the name *Ioudaios* did not end in the first century. Two hundred years later, Bishop Augustine of Hippo knew Christians who still called themselves *Iudaei*, and he explained to them that Christians can and should be called "Israel," but not *Iudaei*. The "Israel" designation debate caused much division; Cohen (1998) argues that "Christians are the true *Judaei* but will create too much confusion if they use that title. Let the Jews have it!" (Cf. Also Dunn, 1992).

The theory has been proposed that Yavneh modified the twelfth clause of the ancient prayer known as the "Eighteen Benedictions," which invoked a curse on heretics in general, and Christians in particular, that ultimately forced Christians to worship outside of the synagogue (Jocz, 1948; Wright, 1992; Moore, 1996). However, there is little historical evidence for Christian "witch-hunting" during the Yavnean period between 70 and 135 CE (Cohen 1984; Katz, 1984; Gafni, 1984, 29f.).

Schurer (1885) argues that it is clear that some Jews cursed Christians during the statutory prayers, however, there is no evidence that Christians were officially barred from synagogues. The *birkat ha-minim* is no "watershed" in the history of the relationship of Jews and Christians, as there was no single edict that caused the irreparable separation between Judaism and Christianity. A Yavnean "conspiracy" to conceal the true identity of Jesus as Israel's Messiah, is inconsistent with the nature of the "cursing"; if there was a curse it ensued from a body of historical information that provided evidence of his Messiahship.

However, the emphasis during the Yavnean period represented a return to a devout study of the Torah (Freyne, 1988), the same Law — in the view of the Yavnean rabbis — from whence Jewish Christians claimed their "freedom" (Neusner, 1996).

Koenig (1979) argues that the rabbis at Yavneh were compelled to draw a distinction between traditional Judaism and that element within the Christian movement that considered itself Jewish. The decision in effect institutionalized the separation of synagogue and church, and no persecutions were decreed. No edict prevented Christians from attending synagogue services. On the contrary, a change, Koenig urges, was introduced into one of the chief synagogue prayers, that is, the "Eighteen Benedictions." The twelfth benediction, notes Koenig, was altered to include Christians and other "heretical" groups in a curse. It appears that the theory was that wherever this new version of the Benedictions was prayed, Jewish Christians could not participate in good conscience. Koenig's view is generally affirmed in the literature.

If a synagogue ruler doubted whether a participant was actually praying the curse, he could call the individual before the Torah *niche* to lead the prayer as a "delegate of the congregation." This was an effective means by the rabbis to force Jewish Christians to stand for their convictions and to decide either for — or against — fellowship in the synagogue.

There is no historical information to indicate the level of acceptance of this prayer in the various synagogues throughout the ancient world. Koenig (1979) argues the new prayer found rapid acceptance in Palestine and Syria, where the rabbinic academy wielded its greatest power. However, Parkes (1960) suggests that by the beginning of the second century, certain portions of the fourth Gospel were probably circulated in Palestine causing increased tensions between the two Judaisms. Clearly, traditional Judaism with its emphasis on Torah study and obedience, and Christianity that proclaimed freedom from the Law a "yoke" of slavery, while similar in their roots, were not doctrinally compatible. Thus, the rabbinic sages at Yavneh who already lacked credibility and administrative power, while prejudicing the Jewish people against Jesus, could not conceal the person and message of Jesus from the Jewish people (cf. Chapter Four). The sages could only formally pronounce an imprecation against all heretics, including Jewish Christians.

The Search For Historical Objectivity: Questions and Problems

IMMEDIATELY WHEN ONE undertakes an historical study, many questions and problems arise, particularly when a study relates to a period of history where primary historical sources are few. A study is further complicated when we are faced with the problem of dating the sources.

As with any historical investigation, there are a number of arguments that historians assume to be evident in the pursuit of objective historical information, and at the risk of making an over-simplified presentation, I would offer but a few: First, one assumption is that historical objectivity and adequate knowledge by which to formulate logical conclusions is *ascertainable*. If this is assumed *a priori* (knowledge before), then it may be argued that the method of historical inquiry is just as objective as other sciences. Historian Marc Block comments:

> I know the mood of my 'man in the street' only through the chart of it, which he himself agrees to draw for me. Because the individual narrowly restricted by his senses and power of concentration, never perceives more than a tiny path of the vast tapestry of events, deeds, and words which form the destinies of a group, and because, moreover, he possesses an immediate awareness of only his own mental state, all knowledge of mankind, to whatever time it applies, will always derive a large part

of its evidence from others. In this respect, the student of the present is scarcely any better off than the historian of the past.[1]

Thus, we are left to the primary sources for a direct account, and secondary sources for interpretation and commentary, for "how are we to understand a faith we do not share except through the accounts of others?"[2] It is this "indirect knowledge" the methodologists have understood in a general sense that arrives at the mind of the historian only by way of other human minds.[3]

Second, historical accounts are *fragmentary*, yet this does not abolish objectivity any more than the absence of a few fossil remains would prevent a geologist from reconstructing a long extinct animal. What is important to understand in this analogy is that a present-day geologist is only reconstructing the "probable", and not actual past. By employing the historical method, the historian weighs the integrity of eyewitness accounts to put the pieces of the historical puzzle together into a "probable" portrait.

The primary sources are few that directly pertain to Yohanan ben Zakkai and Yavneh, with more that bear upon the literary and historical context pertaining to events that immediately follow the Roman War, the effects on Palestine—Judea in particular—and the state of the Jews in the Land.

Third, all historians must *select* their sources, yet the selection of primary historical sources does not make history subjective. The duty of a juror is to make a judgment that transcends "beyond reasonable doubt," and this most often means the juror does not have all the evidence. What is at issue here must necessarily be the access to crucial and relevant evidence in order to arrive at objectivity. Thus, the objectivity of Roman historian Josephus, for example, is not questioned in this study, except if demonstrable contradictions are found.

Fourth, while true that value judgments are the result of language cloaked with values, as Herbert Butterfield demonstrates, this does not make historical objectivity impossible.[4] The goal of the historian is to give definition to the events and their value in the original *historical* and *cultural* context. I would argue that in order to be objective, the historian must make careful value judgments based upon primary documents.

Fifth, the goal of the historian is to ascertain factuality and events sequentially, and not to assume the veracity of one particular interpretation over another. The historian must recognize the line between causal connections and the interpretative framework to understand the facts. It is one matter to understand Yohanan ben Zakkai as a charismatic and strong rabbinical leader who reconstructed first century Judaism, and altogether another matter to assume a sinister design to conceal and therefore defraud the Jewish community of the knowledge of the true Messiah. As this study shall demonstrate, many false "messiahs" came on the scene and departed during the Yavnean period. The Christian movement as a "Judaism" or a doctrinally unified Christology did not enjoy a cohesive orthodoxy until much later.

Last, all historians are products of their own time, and as such, offer some *degree* of objectivity. We must not confuse the content of knowledge with the process of ascertaining it; nor allow for the formulation of a particular view and not judge the merit of its formulation as a separate issue.

Without doubt, the mere idea of "objective truth" is regarded with horror in certain academic circles today. Roger Kimball, managing editor of "The New Criterion," agrees. He writes concerning another widespread tendency to downgrade facts to matters of opinion—"a tendency that follows naturally from the rejection of objective truth."[5] This tendency, Kimball notes, shows itself in the amazingly prevalent assumption that all truth is relative, i.e., that the truth of what is said depends crucially on the interest, prejudices, even the sex or ethnic origin of the speaker, and not the truth or falsehood of what the speaker says.[6]

Thus, in the quest to ascertain truth from extant historical sources, one must allow the objective rules of evidence to prevail. Simon Greenleaf comments on the first rule of evidence: "Every document, apparently ancient, coming from the proper repository or custody, and bearing on its face no evident marks of forgery, the law presumes to be genuine, and devolves on the opposing party the burden of proving it to be otherwise."[7]

On the second rule of evidence, Greenleaf writes, "In matters of public and general interest, all persons must be presumed to be conversant, on the principle that individuals are presumed to be conversant with their own affairs."[8]

By following established rules of evidence, the historian finds objective criteria for evaluation that transcends opinion. On opinion versus "fact", again Kimball observes:

> The irony that attends this triumph of interpretation over facts is that it ultimately undermines opinion just as thoroughly as it undermines fact. When facts are downgraded to opinions, they no longer have the authority of facts; but opinions without the bedrock of facts deliquesce into whims. As Hannah Arendt observed in her essay 'Truth and Politics,' opinion remains opinion only so long as it is grounded in, and can be corrected by fact. 'Facts,' she wrote, 'inform opinions, and opinions, inspired by different interests and passions, can differ widely and still be legitimate as long as they respect factual truth. Freedom of opinion is a farce unless factual information is guaranteed and the facts themselves are not in dispute.'
>
> What are at stake in the confusion of fact and opinion, Arendt concluded, are nothing less than the common world of factual reality and historical truth. It will be pointed out that truth is very often difficult to achieve; that *facts are often hard to establish; that the historical record is incomplete, contradictory, and inaccessible.* Yes. Precisely—but the recalcitrance of truth is all the more reason we need to

remain faithful to the procedures for achieving it: Without them, we are blind.[9]

The appeal to objectivity based upon historical facts, while alone does not guarantee desired outcomes, it reduces subjective interpretation and allows the data to speak for itself.

As theologian N.T. Wright cautions, one must guard against attempting to reconstruct history by studying the much later effects of stories and events. To suggest that a story is biased, Wright observes, "or to suggest that continuing to tell the same story is likely to perpetuate a biased and perhaps violent point of view, is not to say anything one way or another about its historical value."[10]

In fact, the social obligation of the historian to his own day must be balanced with the professional responsibility to follow the evidence wherever it leads. Society is not properly served by suppressing truth or inventing falsehood.[11]

In my view, theories may be proposals to envision things in a certain way as "useful fictions" or "explanatory models". Hypotheses and theories are necessarily (1) *provisional* but still probable due to their nature as having foundation in fact and (2) fitting for they are capable of accounting for the facts.

From Jerusalem to Yavneh
One Man to Lead Them

The Temple

FROM ANCIENT TIMES pilgrims climbed many paths to Jerusalem and to the sacred temple.[1] In distant lands Jews sent their annual tribute, and as they prayed to Yahweh, they imagined Jerusalem as their "holy mountain". All Jews affirmed the faithful city of Jerusalem, though in theology they often differed.[2] Jews in all lands had sung with the psalmist, "Pray for the peace of Jerusalem. May all prosper who seek your welfare!" The first destruction of the temple by the Babylonians in 586 BCE and the subsequent captivity caused Jews to reevaluate their personal relationship with their God. At the time of the destruction of the second temple in 70 CE, the Jews were "an ancient people with an ancient tongue and Scriptures".[3]

Jews of both temple conflagrations had an unshakable memory of the past. Jacob Neusner comments:

> They could look back upon ancient enemies now forgotten by history, and ancient disasters, the spiritual lessons of which illumined current times. People thought that they kept the faith by devotion to the holy city, to the sacred temple, to divinely-ordained rites of service, to the priesthood, to the altar. And many a Jew yearned to see the priests upon their platform, to hear the Levites in their great choir singing the songs of David, to receive

the blessing of the Lord in the temple in Jerusalem. If people thought they kept the faith, they had good reason. What had the Lord commanded of old, which now they did not do? For three sins the ancient temple had fallen—murder, adultery, and idolatry. Now, five centuries later, idolatry was a grotesque memory. Murder and adultery were surely not so common among those whom God had instructed as elsewhere, they supposed. As to ancient Scriptures, were these not studied in the synagogues Sabbath upon Sabbath? But the most certain testimony of all to the enduring covenant was the temple, which stood as the nexus between man and God. Its services bore witness to Israel's enduring loyalty to the covenant and the commandments of Sinai. They saw Jerusalem with the eye of faith, and that vision transformed the city.[4]

The social impact of Judaism upon the Roman system was effected by the transformation of the temple by Herod in the first century. Thousands of workers over a century's time—until the very eve of Jerusalem in 66 CE—carried on the massive temple beautification project. In his eighteenth year as Emperor, Herod ordered reconstruction plans that would conform to Solomon's original tedious dimensions, i.e., sixty cubits in length, by twenty in width, and forty cubits high.[5]

The "business" of the city of Jerusalem centered around—and properly so—the enterprise of the temple. The work of the holy city was in the service of the Most High God, and only few doubted it, one exception was the cloistered community of Essenes that had abandoned the temple in favor of a site near the Dead Sea, who regarded the temple as hopelessly impure and ungodly.[6]

In contrast, the Pharisees relied upon the oral tradition received by Moses at Sinai that directed the priests in spiritual conduct to ultimately make the temple the center of the world. On this point, Neusner observes that the Pharisees taught that in the meantime, the temple sacrifice was the true way to serve God, the way decreed from ancient times. "True, there were other ways believed to be more important, for the prophets had emphasized that sacrifice alone was not enough to reconcile the sinner to a God made angry by unethical or immoral behavior."[7] Historical Judaism had always required ethics, morality, humility and faith—complete loyalty to the covenant that specified priestly animal sacrifices, oil, wine, the incense—all dedicated to the Most High God.

"Not one stone..."

In later centuries, both Jews and Christians would recount the destruction of Jerusalem and its temple in 70 CE with contrasting attitudes. Unlike all other generations, Gentiles and Jews alike would reflect back and condemn the generation of Yohanan ben Zakkai. Within the Christian community and conscience resounded the words of their Lord who wept bitterly over the city, and declared that because of her sin, Israel's house would be "forsaken and desolate."[8]

Further on in the Gospel narratives, as Jesus walked around the temple mount and gestured to the buildings, he said, "You see all these, do you not? Truly I say to you, there will not be left here one stone upon another that will not be thrown down."[9]

The historian Eusebius later echoed the sentiments of both the early church and many patristic writers as to why Jerusalem fell and the temple destroyed:

> Concerning the events, then, that befell the Jews after our Savior's passion and those outcries in which the multitude of the Jews refused condemnation of a robber and murderer but entreated that the Prince of Life should be destroyed, it is superfluous to add to the statement of the historian. Yet it may be proper to mention, also, what things occurred that show the benignity of that All-gracious Providence that had deferred their destruction for forty years after their crimes against Christ. During that time, the greater part of the apostles and disciples,

> James himself, the first bishop there, usually called the brother of our Lord, still surviving and still remaining at Jerusalem, continued the strongest bulwark of the place... presented wonderful prodigies of what was about to happen to those who did not repent; all which having been recorded by the historian already cited, it well deserved to be submitted to the view of our readers.[10]

Thus, through two millennia, Christians have seen Jerusalem as the faithless city, murderer of prophets and the Messiah, and laid waste by God himself.

In similar fashion, through the centuries, Jews have lamented the destruction of their most holy sanctuary:

> On account of our sins we have been exiled from our land, and we have been removed far from our country. We cannot go up to appear and bow down before you, to carry out our duties in your chosen Sanctuary, in the great and holy house upon which your name was called.[11]

For the Jew, the destruction resulted in mass homelessness as the land was trampled under the heel of the Roman conqueror. The Romans, Grayzel observes, had ruthlessly destroyed the fertile fields and the orchards from which the rebels might have drawn sustenance. "It would take many years before the soil could be cultivated again to the same extent as before."[12] Many cities and rural towns had been destroyed, particularly throughout Judea, and thousands of young men enslaved. The fall represented the loss of political rights, for before the war, Jews had enjoyed political independence. Palestine was to be governed by a military representative under the emperor. The fall also deprived the Jews of a central Jewish authority, even more passionately felt by diaspora Jews than those in Palestine.[13]

With the temple destroyed, Jews of the world could no longer look to Palestine, its sages, Sanhedrin, synagogues—for guidance in Hebrew custom and religion.

Like the Psalmist of old in the first captivity, the Palestinian Jews felt tormented by their captors; with passion, her leaders at Yavneh would echo the Psalmist, "If I forget you, O Jerusalem, may my right hand forget her skill. May my tongue cleave to the roof of my mouth, if I do not remember you, if I do not exalt Jerusalem above my chief joy."[14]

Greater still, what followed the destruction of the sanctuary was the loss of Jewish prestige. Before the Roman war, the Jewry of the world held their heads high in their affirmation of a special protection by God. The temple enjoyed an unparalleled reputation as one of the great wonders of the ancient world, and Jewish numbers in gentile lands added respect among the pagan populaces. Grayzel observes:

> People may have disliked them [the Jews] for this very pride, or tried to get rid of them because of the economic competition that they offered, but they did not look down upon them. This, too, was changed by the disastrous war. Pagan priests now said that the Jewish God had been vastly overrated. Others proclaimed that God had abandoned the Jews and that it was, therefore, dangerous to be on their side or to follow them.[15]

As if the humiliation of the destruction was not enough, the annual tithe that the Jews had sent to the temple from distant lands, was by Roman decree, ordered to be sent to the temple of Jupiter in Rome. This deliberate insult humiliated the pride of the Jews in their Most High God, for now they were directed to pay tribute to the Olympian god who presumably had conquered Yahweh and was entitled to be His heir.[16] Pagans derided the Jews and viewed them as a huge joke, and the insult was further aggravated when not only the rebellious Palestinian Jews were forced to pay tribute, but also the diaspora Jews who thought the war was of little concern to them. The *Fiscus Judaicus* was unbearable, and some Jews posed as pagans in order to avoid the Roman tax.

The "sins of this generation" whether declared by Christians or the sages, were the sins of the Jews at the time of the second temple. The Roman perspective was vastly different. The Jews had enjoyed nearly eighty years of independence under the Hasmonaeans, and they were hardened to the notion of the imposition of foreign rule.[17] F.F. Bruce comments:

> The later Hasmonaeans had been oppressive to many of their subjects, but by now their evil deeds were forgotten, and only the fact that they were a native dynasty that had freed Israel from foreign domination was remembered.

In 70 CE, the Jews fought a war in the cause of the one true God, and having lost, later historians both Christian and Jew examined that generation for its sin, "[for] none could believe that the omnipotent God would permit his temple to be destroyed for no reason."[18] Neusner comments on the similarity between the 586 BCE destruction of the temple, and the destruction by imagining himself as a Palestinian Jew of that time:

> The alternative was this: 'Either our fathers greatly sinned, or God is not just.' The choice thus represented no choice at all. 'God is just, but we have sinned, we, but mostly our fathers before us. Therefore all that has come upon us—the famine, the exile, the slavery to pagans—these are just recompense for our own deeds.'[19]

The Origin of the "Zakkai" Clan

Jerusalem's most celebrated rabbi ("lord") on the eve of her fall in 70 CE was Yohanan ben Zakkai. Yohanan (Heb. "the Lord graciously gives") was probably born at the beginning of the common era and died a decade after the destruction of Jerusalem, a remarkably long life for a Palestinian Jew. What were Yohanan's family roots? Historical sources do not specify his origin, and the weight of the evidence is borne out in the name *Zakkai* itself.[20]

The Aramaic equivalent of *Zakkai* is the Hebrew *zaddiq*, i.e., "righteous or upright". The word appears in the Genesis account of Noah: "These are the generations of Noah. Noah was a *righteous man*, blameless in his generation." [21]

Both Ezra and Nehemiah, in describing the return of the Jews from Babylon, mentioned *zakkai* in reference to a clan that returned to the land as "the sons of *Zakkai*, seven hundred and sixty," a family of commoners, "the men and people of Israel."[22] The Scripture does not include the sons of Zakkai among the priests, Levites, temple servants, singers, gatekeepers or other distinguished individuals. Neusner believes that the clan was formidable, numbering no less than seven hundred and fifty members.[23]

Rabbinic literature records other individuals named *Zakkai*, for in 200 CE, Rabbi Zakkai, a contemporary of Judah the Prince, is described, along with a Babylonian Amora in the third century, one R. Zakkai who emigrated to Israel.

Herod

Yohanan ben Zakkai's father lived through most of Herod's reign. He was a tyrant who was cruel to the Jews and would at once destroy first born infants to thwart a potential messiah figure who, in his twisted mind, might incite Jewish hatred towards Roman domination.[24] Herod exerted imperial rule through the use of territorial monarchs and puppet kings who lorded over hostile regions which could not safely receive a Roman viceroy.

In other areas, such as Celicia and Armenia, Rome affirmed or supported kings friendly to the Empire, and ethnarchs and tetrarchs governed in lands where Rome would not choose to rule. Herod was quite an efficient ruler who levied taxes, initiated public works projects which developed lands and reduced unemployment. Yet no other building project bearing his name would be more remembered than the great temple in Jerusalem.[25]

Herod employed vast multitudes to construct several cities and palaces that encompassed the magnificent Herodian in the South, Sebaste in Samaria, and the beautiful port city of Caesarea. Where the earlier Hasmonean monarchs had promulgated political turmoil, Herod had succeeded in stabilizing Palestinian life as a whole with minimal political manipulation. After all, where palace murders of potentially harmful wives, servants, and sons were carried out in casual fashion, "politics" was redefined. Under Herod, the Sanhedrin was an ignored institution, and culture was in essence Hellenistic domination. Jews were manifestly forbidden to participate in all Roman public affairs and political life was merely an instrument of the state.[26]

The destruction of the temple gave a new vision and impetus to Yohanan to begin a reformulation of Judaism. Where Rome succeeded in taking Jews away from their sacred temple, the Romans failed to remove the temple from the heart of the Jew. Thus, the Jewish faith that Rome could not destroy and would be redefined at Yavneh a decade later under Yohanan, a five-fold reaffirmation that had long since been instituted in the temple system.

First, Judaism itself and Jewish custom survived imperial Roman slaughter. The Jewish concept of the unity of God, the commandments of God, and covenant relationships were not physical instruments that could be destroyed, but were the essence of the Jewish soul, a spiritual soul that would elude the Romans in their quest for the ideal state. Grayzel comments:

> The customs which had grown up during the previous centuries were also not subject to death by the sword. Such were the obligation to rest on the Sabbath, the custom of observing as holy the days upon which important events had taken place, the dietary laws and any number of other traditions within and outside the Jewish home. These traditions were not connected with the temple or with national life, but they were widespread, being observed wherever Jews lived.[27]

Second, the Torah — the "teaching" — of Judaism could not be destroyed. From the time of Ezra, Jews had viewed study as central to Jewish custom and identity. The "love of study", the quest for knowledge for its own sake by Jews was universal, whether study undertaken by peasants of the written law, or that undertaken by the educated of the unorganized Oral Law that would be codified under Yohanan ben Zakkai and Gamaliel II at Yavneh. "This love of study was universal among the Jews. Rome could not destroy all the books in Jewish possession, and certainly not the desire to study them."[28]

Third, the institution of the synagogue remained intact, for by 70 CE, synagogues existed in vast numbers throughout the Roman Empire. While Rome destroyed many synagogues in rebellious Palestine, synagogues in the outer regions continued unmolested; all things considered, to Jews the synagogue building itself was unimportant, but the prayers, recitation of psalms, traditions, and social connections were valued above all else.

Fourth, Rome could never destroy the cherished memories that all Jews shared of the past, particularly the monarchy under Kings David and Solomon. This gave Jews a sense of pride and prevented them from being assimilated by the pagans among whom they lived.[29]

Last, during the Herodian period, expectations of Messiah flowed deep within the Jewish conscience. The idea of a superhuman, a founder of national righteousness that would touch all nations under one supreme Ruler, took hold in the imagination of the Jewish people, "and helped to make their sad lot more tolerable [through] hopes for a happy future."[30]

Pre-Jewish War Economy

Taxes levied by the Romans were targeted toward men, houses, sales, animals, exports, and imports. In addition to these taxes, the ancient faith of the Jews imposed the tithe that supported the temple Levites, offerings, and animal sacrifices. Jews regarded Roman taxes as robbery for they saw Roman occupation and rule as illegitimate.[31]

Roman authority allowed many Jews to take advantage of vast enterprises in travel and commerce, and numbers of Jews settled in remote corners of the Roman empire. Among those who stayed in Palestine in order to benefit from the *pax romana* that extended to economic stability was Yohanan ben Zakkai.

The Midrash Tannaim, in superlative Mosaic language, records that Yohanan was a tradesman: "One hundred and twenty years he lived. Forty years he spent in business, forty years he studied, and forty years he sustained all Israel."[32]

As with the origin of Yohanan's name and birth, the nature and scope of his enterprise is unknown, though one source of evidence indicates that he understood the fundamentals and practices of business. The Mishnah records a discussion in which Yohanan voiced his concern over dishonest weights and measures.[33]

Palestinian living standards for the populace in general, and Jews in particular, were modest. Among Jews in the first century, archaeology has failed to uncover ornate synagogues, treasures, expensive pottery, or rich sarcophagi. The general peasantry ate inexpensive foods, among which were bread made from poor quality wheat, highly salted fish, and other low quality grain from Egypt, such as barley. Diluted beer or wine was consumed, and fish was served on the Sabbath. Few people were involved in national or international commerce, most being content as farmers or tradesmen. The teaching parables of Jesus drew heavily on farming metaphors (The Sower), trade (Lost Coin), and fishing (The Net).[34]

Jewish Education

Education among all Jewish classes focused on the main disciplines of Jewish tradition, religious learning, especially rote learning of the Holy Scriptures. Creation of the world by God was assumed, and lessons about Abraham, Isaac, Jacob and Joseph, Moses and the Law, and ethical teaching of the prophets formed the foundation of Jewish study. The Torah of Moses gave the community of faith the basis for conducting its affairs both within its social structure and with non-Jews. In a practical sense, Jews received instruction about how to relate to the helpless and homeless, the stranger and outsider. All Jews were instructed that God is one and that there are no other gods before Yahweh.[35]

The prophets, they were told, warned of pending disasters if Israel disobeyed the Lord's covenant laws. What was absolutely ingrained within the Jewish conscience was that despite conquest and conquerors, whether Pharaoh Shishak in 586 BCE, or Vespasian and Titus in 70 CE, the God of Abraham guided His covenant people and that all things happened within God's decree. So they were taught to look for the meaning of daily and cosmic events alike. A comet, drought, broken leg, or earthquake—all could equally convey a truth. In the biblical writings they studied the wisdom of ancient sages, learning prudence, piety, and understanding. In modern terms their curriculum included much attention to matters of metaphysics, law and morality, ethics and history. Such lessons were intended to create a decent human being.[36]

Similarly, the ancient Greeks had in effect asked, "What is a human being? How should we then live?" The ethical teachings of Hillel, Jesus, then later Yohanan ben Zakkai and Gamaliel II all echoed both the primacy of a personal relationship between God and man, and the highest regard for fellow human beings.

Jewish Social Structures

The fact that the regions in Palestine were by nature distinctive and variable, social structures were further made complicated, for while Jerusalem was the urban center for Jews, the population was comprised of varied levels of classes: absentee landlords, wealthy merchants, and priests who lived on temple endowments.[37] In addition, since the temple required the skills of various artisans, these craftsmen, along with traders, urban proletariat and unskilled laborers crowded the streets of Jerusalem.

Judean provincials were less likely to respect the ritual requirements for cleanliness, and for this reason, Jerusalemites would tend to separate from them and purified themselves for the festal pilgrimage. Judean provincials usually had little advanced education, and friction between rural and urban residents was extensive. Country landowners and peasantry were themselves divided.

Yohanan, business entrepreneur and rabbi, filled the void of rural farmers and proletarian that were divorced from the main issues that concerned Palestine. The Jewish population welcomed strong personalities, especially sages possessed by vast learning.[38] In the first century, there were many "Judaisms" within Judaism, as evidenced by the Essenes, Pharisees, Sadducees, Zealots, Sicarri, the Fourth Philosophy, Therapeutae, Samaritans, various Christian sects, and others. While sectarianism marked Pre-war Palestine, after 70 CE, historic Judaism was not marked by sectarianism.[39] Samaritans continued to exist as a fringe group, and the Christian population became mostly gentile and would ultimately become a separate religion altogether.

Josephus was both a Roman general and Jew, but as a Jew, he paid little notice to the community life of Israel in his extensive narrative of war and politics. While the masses of people turned away from politics, a few indicated their disapproval of the course of events by withdrawing from ordinary society.[40] Some became hermits, while others fled to neighboring lands, or entered ascetic communities similar to the Essenes on the banks of the Dead Sea. Essenic purification rites required that they prepare for Armageddon and the final battle against impiety, sin, and evil. The Essenes affirmed:

> This is the regulation for the men of the commune, who devote themselves to turn away from all evil, and to hold fast to all that he has commanded as his will, to separate themselves from the congregation

of men of iniquity to be a commune in Torah and property.[41]

The separatists of the first century were arguably the Pharisees, who believed that the world was in disorder. The way they chose identified with ordinary society, as taught by Hillel who believed that they should not be separate from the community of faith.[42] The Pharisees desired to build society up from the ruins, and while differing among themselves with some focusing on the spiritual welfare of the nation, the Zealots sought to re-store the grandeur of Israel through rebellion and war. Josephus comments:

> ...they are able greatly to influence the masses of the people. Whatever the people do about divine worship, prayers, and sacrifices, they perform ac-cording to their direction. The cities give great praise to them on account of their virtuous con-duct, both in the action of the their lives and their teachings also.[43]

While Josephus may have exaggerated the extent of the Pharisee's power, they certainly exerted some influ-ence in the religious life of Israel before they finally came to power in 70 CE. "By keeping the rules of purity," notes Neusner, "the fellow separated from the common man. But by remaining within the towns and cities of the land, he preserved the possibility of teaching others by exam-ple." This was the Judaic tradition promulgated by Hillel and passed to his disciple, Yohanan ben Zakkai.[44]

The Sadducees were conservative in both belief and ritual, and stood for strict adherence of the written word in all religious matters, acknowledging Scripture as sole revelation and themselves as arbiters of that revelation. They denied the ancient traditions attributed to Moses, and claimed as fallacious the Pharisaic notion of the re-ality of Scripture and oral tradition. Where the Phari-sees believed in the eternality of the soul, bodily revival through resurrection, judgment, and life in the world to come, the Sadducees saw little in Scripture to support such doctrines. Neusner comments:

> In their day however the Sadducees claimed to be the legitimate heirs of Israel's faith. Holding positions of power and authority, they succeeded in leaving so deep an impression on society that even their Pharisaic, Essenic, and Christian opponents did not wholly wipe out their memory.[45]

Where the Sadducees discovered their greatest influence among merchants and landowners, Pharisees gravitated to the lower classes; the Essenes drew adherents from among the disenchanted of all classes. Yohanan was a Pharisee after the tradition of Hillel, but he either acquired or innately possessed Essenic tendencies, particularly in his pacifist view towards Roman occupation.[46]

Rome and Jewish Autonomy

Baron and Juster have well documented how imperial Rome was careful to recognize and respect Jewish self-rule, for the populace was accountable to Jewish law with conflicts adjudicated by Jewish prefects.[47] Rome's indifference to the affairs of the Jewish people did not preclude its own objectives and purposes, however, the empire's policies were often effected without totalitarian methods. In addition, the High Court, known also as the Sanhedrin, had some freedom to determine religious expression of local law and cult.[48]

Once Judea became a part of the administration of Syria, the Sanhedrin could not impose the death penalty.[49] It is not clear if the Sanhedrin ever had authority to impose the death penalty during Herod's reign as Alon suggests, yet they did have autonomy to maintain temple affairs.[50] The Sanhedrin maintained the following functions:

(1) Decisions in commercial/civil law.
(2) Defined family and personal status and marriage procedure.

(3) Collected biblical levies; determined the sacred calendar.[51]

(4) Sadducees and Pharisees administrated the social, religious, and economic life of Israel.

The Sanhedrin provided a means to formulate and implement these interests. The leaders of both major opinions played a considerable part in its autonomy. The exact nature of Jewish institutions and self-government that formed a part of it was yet to be implemented. The modern historian's task is further complicated as the sources are difficult, and no body of sources presents a single picture that can be objectively verified in some other independent tradition.[52]

According to the Rabbinic tradition in the Talmud, Hillel the Elder, along with his colleague Shammai, received the Torah from Shemaiah and Avtalion, and passed it on to Yohanan ben Zakkai. Yohanan entered a world of two conflicting worldviews. The first view was that of his own people that an eternal God stood outside of His creation and made human beings in His own image. The second worldview saw the value of the individual purely in relationship to the Roman State. The "gods" of imperial Rome were flawed and mirrored super humans who often ruled through personal whim and deceit. The teachings of Yohanan viewed universals as discoverable and absolute, whereas "truth" in the Roman system of *pax romana* was pragmatic. On virtually all theological and philosophical grounds the two systems were opposed to each other.[53]

Hillel and Shammai

According to the Talmud, Yohanan ben Zakkai took over from Hillel and Shammai, having received from them the tradition concerning God, the world, and man.[54] The tradition held that God was personal and that he created the world, explained his will to man, and that the Scripture was God's means to communicate his will and plan to mankind. The Torah was not only God's source for instruction of Yahweh's will, but the very Word of God that breathed life to Israel's community of faith.[55]

Prior to the temple's destruction, the Pharisees oversaw only their own affairs through a central institution that included the main factions within the Pharisaic sect. At the beginning of the Common Era, both Hillel and Shammai led the Pharisaic community, and upon Hillel's death, his son Gamaliel I replaced him.[56] Neusner contends that Simeon ben Gamaliel and Yohanan ben Zakkai succeeded approximately two decades before the Jewish rebellion of 66-70 CE:

> I cannot date these events with any degree of close accuracy, but suggest the sequence of Yohanan's life on the basis of the little evidence available. The only certain date is 70 CE, by which time Yohanan was certainly at Yavneh.[57]

Because the disciples of Hillel mainly wrote the Mishnah, the actual extant sayings of Shammai are few in number and incomplete.[58] Scholars agree that Yohanan probably did not study with Shammai, and the three clear Scriptural exegeses that he left behind do not indicate a consistent method. Common among all sages of that period was a characteristic emphasis on the happiness of studying Torah. Shammai had said, "Fix a period for your study of the Torah. Say little and do much, and receive all men with a cheerful countenance." In that same spirit, Yohanan taught his disciples.[59]

The tradition affirms that Yohanan was Hillel's disciple, having come to Jerusalem from Babylonia around 30 BCE, and died in Jerusalem around 85 CE. Hillel taught a hermeneutic that changed Pharisaic intellectual life. These principles are also familiar to scholars of Greek classics:

(1) Inference *a minori ad majus;*
(2) Inference by analogy;
(3) Constructing a family on the basis of one passage(extending a specific regulation of

one biblical passage to a number of passages);

(4) The same rule as the preceding, constructing a family on the basis of two biblical passages;

(5) The General and the Particular, the Particular and the General;

(6) Exposition by means of another, similar passage; and

(7) Deduction from the context.[60]

What is remarkable by means of comparison between Hillel, Yohanan, and Jesus is that the Hillelite exegesis "extended the potentialities of interpreting a given text in many ways. They thus made possible a very broad and liberal interpretation of Scripture." [61] The sayings of Hillel reveal a remarkably humble man:

Be of the disciples of Aaron, loving peace and pursing it, loving thy fellow-creatures, and drawing them near to the Torah. A name made great is a name destroyed. [62]

Hillel always stressed the importance continual learning:

He who does not increase his knowledge diminishes it. He who does not study deserves to die. He who makes profane use of the crown of Torah will waste away.[63]

Hillel's most notable saying echoes Jesus: "If I am not for myself, who will be for me? But when I am for myself alone, what am I? And if not now, when?"[64] According to Hillel, study transcended information about the world and cosmos: study of Torah was the key to eternal life, included insight to the foundations of all reality, and contained keys to the universe itself.

Hillel held a platonic view of material possessions, a notion that wealth was an impediment to man's quest for knowledge and truth that merely substitutes worries and concerns about the imperfect world of the temporary. Because men would ultimately receive their fair reward, Hillel taught that men should not join those of little faith who worry about the necessities of the world. In similar fashion, Jesus addressed the same concerns regarding wealth and worry (Matthew 6:16-24; 25-34). At Yavneh, Yohanan ben Zakkai would restate his Master Hillel in contemporary language that would reformulate historic Judaism.

Yohanan's master taught his disciple to dedicate himself to the ideal of peace: "Be of the disciples of Aaron, loving peace, pursuing peace, loving mankind, and drawing all men to Torah."[65] The master also taught Yohanan the supreme Commandment to "Love the Lord your God with all your heart, with all your soul, with all your mind, and with all your strength," and this passion of Torah study would lead Yohanan at Yavneh to reformulate Judaism in the light of that revelation. However, at Yavneh, the *Birkat ha-Minim* pronouncement ("Blessing") would in time exclude Jewish Christians from the synagogue and redefine Judaism to exclude Jewish believers in Jesus.

The Academy at Yavneh, ca. 70—85 CE

The reformulation and reestablishment of Judaism in Palestine after the destruction of Jerusalem was necessarily bound up in the personality of Yohanan ben Zakkai, the leading Pharisee who mitigated disputes between his own party and the Sadducees, and chief deputy under Simon ben Gamaliel who was head of the Sanhedrin after the expulsion of Cestius Gallus from Jerusalem.[66] It is not certain that Yohanan, unlike Gamaliel, may have refused to take part in the Jewish revolt for the pursuit of peace was paramount in his teachings. What is certain is that Yohanan exhorted the rebels to moderate their behavior towards gentiles.

A saying attributed to Yohanan was this: "Do not haste to tear down altars of gentiles, lest you be forced to rebuild them with your own hands, lest you tear down altars of bricks and be ordered to build them of stone."[67] Another saying was, "If you hold a sapling in your hand

and someone says to you the Messiah is there, plant the sapling first and then welcome the Messiah."[68] It appears that Yohanan had a realistic attitude and a general distrust of apocalyptic enthusiasm.

In the absence of a national Jewish state, the spiritual existence of Israel had to be redefined, and the process involved the creation of the Beth Din, or the High Court. Yohanan was directly involved with this development from about 70 to 85 CE. Upon his death, Rabban Gamaliel II took the lead well into the first quarter of the second century.[69]

George Foote Moore comments on the importance of the Academy at Yavneh:

> There was an urgent need of a body competent to determine matters of the utmost importance to all Jews, foremost among which was the fixing of the calendar with the correct dates of all the festivals and fasts, for which the law prescribed days certain as of the essence of the observance. Innumerable questions arose also from the cessation of the Temple worship, for which there was no rule or precedent, and about which an authoritative decision was necessary if there was not to be endless perplexity of conscience and confusion of practice.[70]

The Beth Din at Yavneh was a far different body of rabbis than that of the Great Sanhedrin in Jerusalem that enjoyed both spiritual oversight and political collaboration with the Roman authorities. While the Sanhedrin was a national council under the watchful eye of the Roman procurator, having political powers and obligations, the Beth Din was a tenuous leadership council that presided over legal affairs within the confines of rabbinic Judaism.[71] The high priest was head of the Sanhedrin that comprised itself of the aristocracy, and the lay leaders were allied with them sharing Sadducean tendencies.[72] George Foote Moore contends that in the Sanhedrin party the Sadducees were the dominant party,[73] however, other scholars believe that the Pharisees had the upper hand.[74]

The data seems to indicates that Yohanan, as leader of the Pharisees, constantly debated with the Sadducees over many issues and won, for Yohanan's disciples and peers were *all* Pharisees; as Ginzberg observes, the rabbinical council was *exclusively* Pharisaic.[75]

While Yohanan brought the reorganization of Judaism back to the dominant Pharisaism, a more thorough reorganization would take place after the second war of 132-135 CE. The second reorganization would regulate the rabbinic teaching office, the Jewish canon, and draw a clear distinction between fringe groups such as Christianity.

The question we must ask is this: What was the state of Jewish economic conditions, both collectively and personal, following the first war against Rome? The final results of the Jewish disaster in 70 CE, observes Conzelmann, indicates that the status of the Jews remained unchanged in the Greco-Roman Empire. It is unlikely that there was any acute severing of relations with Jewish Hellenism, for outside the conflagration in Palestine, the status of Jews was undamaged even though the Romans prohibited Jews from practicing circumcision.

Neusner observes that post-war Palestine suffered dramatically, with widespread famine and economic depression.[76] In spite of the circumcision prohibition by Roman decree, with the desolation of Palestine in general and Judea in particular, Judaism and Jewish social life continued unhindered.[77]

Schurer, Vermes and Millar have meticulously documented the process of Roman Hellenization that continued in Palestine itself that influenced the production of literature in the Hellenistic style.[78] Jews freely moved about unhindered in their travels and settlements, and grew in large numbers, particularly in Galilee, Rome and Babylon.[79]

Yohanan ben Zakkai, though a pacifist towards Rome, gained the adoration of his countrymen, and established himself as *Rabban* — "dear Lord" — of his people. In the wake of the calamity that destroyed the temple, Yohanan needed to initiate an act of leadership, for both he and his colleagues had always claimed a "sole legitimacy" as spiritual leaders of the people.[80] The town of Yavneh in the year 70 CE provided Yohanan the impetus for asserting his authority:

> In their hands alone, they held, were the Scriptures and Oral Traditions inseparably revealed to Moses long ago. But how did he demonstrate that this was so? Those who formerly had heard the Pharisaic claim ignored it. The best way to win their attention was to make a decree and to forcefully effect it. What of the opposition? Priests survived the cataclysm [fall of Jerusalem]. Remnants of the other groups and sects were still much in evidence. Yohanan looked for an occasion publicly and dramatically both to assert his authoritative position and to force the opposition to accept it. The hour was not long in coming. It came on the new Year, probably the month following the temple's destruction...[81]

We must now turn to the question, what position in fact, did Yohanan hold *from the public perspective* during the time of his leadership? Did the people both accept his authority and regard him as a spokesman for the best interests of the people, as some modern scholars suggest, thus enabling Yohanan to conceal the identity of Jesus and the new Nazarene movement? [82]

While historians consider possible answers,[83] the essential question had nothing to do with Yohanan's *title*, but rather his *function*. Was Yohanan's performance, in any degree, duties that characterize the Patriarchate (Patriarch) after him, demonstrating that he was both president of the Sanhedrin and Israel's leader? Scholars almost universally answer this question in the affirmative.[84]

Evidence from the Mishnah suggests, however, that Yohanan's leadership was not universally affirmed, but that Sadducean elements opposed him, inferring that perhaps they (the Sadducees) believed that they were the rightful leaders. One indication from the Mishnah may lead one to conclude the preceding:

> Rabbi Judah said that Ben Bukhri testified at Yavneh, that a priest who paid the shekel [Temple tax, from which he was exempt] did not thereby commit a sin. Said Rabban Yohanan ben Zakkai to him: On the contrary, any priest who did not pay the shekel was guilty of a sin. The only thing is, the priests interpret Scripture to their own advantage. The verse (Lev 6:16) 'Every meal-offering of the priest shall be wholly burned, it shall not be eaten' they expound as follows: If the Omer, and the Two Loaves and the shewbread are ours [paid for in part by one shekel] how can they be eaten? [thus, no tax].[85]

Along with the element among the Sadducees towards Yohanan's position at Yavneh, a considerable number of Priests, prominent both before the destruction and after, seem not to have participated in Yohanan's Academy. Notably among them was Rabbi Nehunya ben Haqaneh.[86] This is quite remarkable because he is mentioned in the Tradition as a disciple of Yohanan.[87] Many others were conspicuously absent from participation.[88]

It appears from the records that the most pressing problem facing the rabbinic authorities at Yavneh were matters of liturgy, or worship. During the former years of the temple, days and festivals were observed as part of the sacrificial cult; Yohanan was now pressed to decree a series of specific modifications of law, necessitated by the disaster.[89] Goldin observes that later Yohanan, and his successors, would define the authority of the academy that issued these ordinances at an earlier date, claiming that the academy held the same authority once exerted by the Sanhedrin in Jerusalem.[90]

The High Court at Yavneh was now the Beth Din with the full affirmation to issue binding enactments. "Yohanan's method was that of Hillel, Gamaliel I, and Simeon ben Gamaliel before him: to issue decrees of specific legal problems." [91]

Sects that opposed the new coalition were greatly weakened by the war, if not totally disbanded. Cerinthians and Ebionites were virtually destroyed or scattered abroad, while the Christians escaped to Pella in the Transjordan. The Herodians fled to distant gentile lands,[92] and the Essenes were apparently destroyed.[93]

The Pharisees attained and maintained popular recognition, having the upper hand in the reformulation of Judaism; Sadducees, on the other hand, held to unpopular doctrines and their social position was tenuous. In addition, they groped with ensuing problems associated with the destruction, having few if any answers to provide the people for the temple's downfall.[94]

The Pharisees enjoyed numerous advantages over all other sects in general, and the Sadducees in particular. Neusner notes that they advanced a comprehensive religious plan to replace the fallen sacrificial system.[95] Second, their hermeneutical principles allowed them to interpret Torah law in a more liberal construction, and due to the changing circumstances that affected Jerusalem and Judaism, this carried important pragmatic considerations relating to administration and public policies.[96]

Third, the dogmas of the Pharisees better addressed the peasant concerns that surrounded the question of why righteous people must suffer evil at the hands of the unrighteous gentiles. They had clear statements concerning providence, retribution, life beyond death, and recompense for suffering. Fourth, the nation as a whole gave broad affirmation to the Pharisees due to their pacifist war policy.

Fifth, the Romans gave their confidence to the Pharisees because of the loyalty of many sages towards Roman law. Sixth, with the fall of Jerusalem, the Pharisees advanced their prior claim as the sole interpreters of Judaism. All of these elements set the historical stage for Yohanan ben Zakkai to assume his rightful role as "Rabban" at Yavneh. In Yohanan's judgment, he and his disciples had both the right and obligation to reformulate the religious and social order of Judaism.[97]

The actual achievements and policies attributed to Yohanan ben Zakkai are delineated in the Mishnah. The question asked before remains: Does the actual historical record reveal that there was a deliberate attempt by the sages to conceal the "messianic identity of Jesus" from the Jewish people?

Virtually all historical investigation into the achievements of Yohanan ben Zakkai agree that the founding of the Academy at Yavneh, thriving for well over a century, along with the Beth Din that inherited many of the functions of the defunct Sanhedrin, was an incredible achievement.[98]

The Mishnah provides no historical information about the Academy of Yohanan ben Zakkai, whether disciples, method of instruction, or what branches of Torah tradition that was emphasized.[99] We do have evidence that Yohanan's impetus was heavy in the instructional aspects of the Academy, for he had great concern that the oral Torah taught by the Pharisees would not be forgotten,[100] and that the spiritual and social needs of the ordinary person would receive attention by trained scholars.[101]

Another important achievement of Yohanan at Yavneh was the founding of the Beth Din, and his acts as president which will be discussed at below. Alon and Neusner both emphasize that there should be no sharp distinction between the Great Academy and the Beth Din, for those scholars who were members of the Academy were also court members.[102]

As a result of the rebellion, the High Court at Yavneh was stripped of its judicial autonomy. In fact, it dealt with no actual law-cases, having sole authority to administrate religious affairs only within the confines of the community of faith.[103] The Tradition outlines the policies and enactments of Yohanan and his High Court in Rosh Hashanah 4:1-4, and Sukkah 3:12. With the sole exception of one passage, all historical narratives deal with the laws of Rosh Hashanah and the method of determining the New Moon of Tishri.

As supreme rabbi following the destruction, Yohanan took careful and calculated steps to fill the spiritual void which the temple's destruction had wrought upon the people. For Yohanan, it was as though he relived the Babylonian exile echoed by the Psalmist:

> By the rivers of Babylon we sat and wept when we remembered Zion. There on the poplars we hung our harps, for there our captors asked us for songs, our tormentors demanded songs of joy; they said, 'Sing us one of the songs of Zion!'... If I forget you, O Jerusalem, may my right hand forget its skill. May my tongue cling to the roof of my mouth if I do not remember you, if I do not consider Jerusalem my highest joy.[104]

Thus, for Yohanan's, "greatest joy" was nearly an obsession that had a twofold dimension: First, to keep a passion for Torah learning alive in and through his disciples; and second, to perpetuate through all generations certain temple rituals. This transfer to the ordinary Jewish home and local synagogue what had always been exclusively temple ritual, was to continue in essence the Feast of Tabernacles.[105]

Most significantly, however, the sages wanted to preserve Jewish continuity of religious expression in the wake of the devastation of Jerusalem, with a reformulation that would follow all Jews in the dispersion. The sages firmly believed that the present Roman occupation was merely temporary in its nature and scope, thus they affirmed: "Speedily will the [temple] be rebuilt."[106]

In the wake of the disaster, the sages were compelled to address a theological question: with the temple destroyed, "What would a convert do if there were no sacrifices?" [The solution to this did not come in Yohanan's time, but was still debated much later during the time of rabbis Eliezer and Joshua.[107]]

Alon observes that nascent Christianity believed that the destruction of Jerusalem was evidence of the a new revelation in Jesus of Nazareth:

Indeed, the very fact that so many of the *mitzvoth* were now no longer capable of observance was held up as proof that Judaism had come to the end of its road. It was now impossible to fulfil the commandments connected with the Temple. Hence, it was argued, the rest of the Jewish Law was finished, too. And although I do not believe that Gentile Christianity played a significant role in Palestine at that time, either numerically or with respect to its impact on the Jewish population — it certainly did not evoke much reaction from the Sages — nevertheless, one may safely assume that it was a factor in the counter-thrust towards preserving these Jewish observances.[108]

What, therefore, does the Mishnah Tradition record regarding the ordinances and enactments of Yohanan at Yavneh? From the historical record, the policies may be organized into three groups:

First, the priestly offerings and privileges. Second, the celebration of the New Moon and festivals and on receiving testimony concerning accurate dates. Third, the disposition of the emoluments of the fallen temple and Jerusalem, along with the proselyte's offering and the fourth-year fruits.[109] In the historical context of what the sages knew and believed about Jesus of Nazareth during the Yavnean period, particularly during the tenure of Yohanan, the *birkat-ha minim* malediction will be later addressed in detail.[110] Regarding these categories, Neusner comments:

> None of the categories reveals decisions on legal matters, but rather on strictly religious questions, which the Romans were probably content to leave to an autonomous Jewish court even during the first years after the destruction. All of them were clearly made necessary by the change in the liturgical situation after the destruction and did not represent innovations in law, so much as modifica-

tions in the face of the new and radically changed circumstances.[111]

The ordinance of the priestly benediction, such as sounding of the *Shofar* on the New Year, caused direct conflict between Yohanan and the priests, as it was a direct imposition of his rabbinic authority over them. In accordance with Exodus 30:21, formerly the priests were not allowed to go onto the platform in the temple to bless the people. Yohanan now required the priests to bless the congregation outside of the temple. In this act, Yohanan was not attempting to prevent the priests from using their former political clout and the power of the blessing to wield a hold over the local congregations in the same manner they had held control in Jerusalem.[112]

In typical pharisaic character that sought identification with the common Jewish peasant, Yohanan emphasized the needs of the congregation over that of the priest, that the congregation is holier, and as Moses removed his shoes before the bush, the priest must remove his shoes before going near the congregation. Thus, Yohanan's act made the priestly blessing inseparable with a divine community of faith, not merely a blessing to be enacted as the priest perceived it; this service-act, again in pharisaic style that emulated Torah, involved washing for purification.[113]

Yohanan dealt openly toward ritual purity with the same tenacity that he dealt with the issue of priestly service. The classic *Halakhah*[114] may be derived from a number of Mishnah passages, and the policy made the laws of ritual purity applicable to the common Jewish peasant only in context of the Sanctuary, and the eating of sacred foods.[115]

Most scholars agree that soon after August of 70 CE, Yohanan attempted to fill the spiritual void caused by the destruction of the temple by decreeing a memorial to the temple itself. The decree carried the *lulav*[116] all seven days, to memorialize the temple. A short time later, probably in the spring of 71, Yohanan issued a second decree more strict in scope, particularly on the Day of Waving, to once again memorialize the temple. He immediately decreed that the people would continue to observe all contingent commandments of the temple, though it lay in ruins, that the festival of Tabernacles would be preserved and observed, and other minor commandments.[117]

Additional ordinances were in similar fashion, which indicate that Yohanan considered the destruction of the temple as an impetus to reinstate older laws that were formerly abolished. Testimony regarding the New Moon of the New Year might be brought the entire day on which the testimony was to be heard, however, the Sabbath might not be profaned in connection with bringing such testimony except for the new year and the month in which Passover came.[118]

Therefore, Yohanan attempted to give to his High Court the prerogatives that up until that time had been reserved to the sanctuary, -to preserve the memory and holiness of the temple. Additionally, the enactments provided for the "temporary" inaccessibility to the temple, as well. In all, nine enactments are preserved in the Traditions: the Shofar; (2) the lulav; (3) the Day of Waving; (4) receiving testimony on the evening of the New Year; (5) receiving testimony even when the head of the court is absent; (6) not profaning the Sabbath to give such testimony, except for the New Year and Passover; (7) the priestly blessing; (8) the proselyte's offering; and (9) the fourth-year fruits.[119]

Neusner purports that it would be unreasonable to assume that the enactments aforementioned were the only actions taken by the High Court, but "what is preserved of his legal record clearly represents what the members of the (later) court of Gamaliel II saw fit to recall."[120] Here again, we must be cautious that whatever is known about Yohanan ben Zakkai — his policies, enactments, and achievements — is ascertained from historical records written *long after* the events. Neusner comments:

> They recalled what they could believe about him, and they could believe only what made sense in their own situation. People did not keep alive traditions, sayings, or stories because they were anti-

quarians, but because they thought them holy or important. A story was a precedent, and a precedent was binding... So the few ordinances we have are those that Gamaliel II and his court transmitted or were unable to suppress.[121]

The Condemnation of "Heretical" writings

Apparently, two separate and distinct groups continue to exist in Judaic studies pertaining to the issue of the acceptance or rejection of the "writings of the heretics" among Yavnean sages. The same two groups view the liturgical emendations of the Eighteen Benedictions by the Yavnean sages as either early – or late – alterations, as pertaining to Yohanan (ca. 80-85 CE), or Gamaliel II (ca. 132 CE).

At the risk of over simplification, I would suggest that there are two variant conclusions by two groups of scholars over the years that may be summarized as follows:

1. Mainly early scholars (1880-1949: Schurer, Jocz, G.F. Moore, Sigal, Parkes, Alon, Herford, Martyn, *et al.*) who identify the "writings of the heretics" as those of early Christian Gospels – and Possibly Pauline epistles – in circulation in Palestine. These scholars identify the "birkat ha-minim" as a malediction towards "all heretics" in general (Ebionites, Gnostics, etc.) and Christians in particular. Thus, they view the debated "nozrim" as peculiar to a Christian designation, and affirm R. Yohanan ben Zakkai as the main initiator of an overall attempt to ban Christians. Additionally, scholars in this school generally view the expulsion of Christians from the synagogue as an early phenomenon (ca 80-120 CE), and mainly instigated by non-Christian Jewish leaders.

2. Predominantly later scholars (1960 to 1999 Neusner, S.D. Cohen, Kimmelman, Horn-

bury, Wilson, Dunn, Setzer, *et al.*) who conclude that the "writings of the heretics" encompassed all non-canonical writings, and that the historical evidence is weak to suggest that Christian texts were included. These scholars view the "birkat ha-minim" as a pronouncement against all "heretics" in general, that the historical accounts in the Talmud are too scant and late and would, therefore, force a "Christian" conclusion. Indeed, a later emendation to the Eighteen Benedictions would suggest Gamaliel II and not Yohanan ben Zakkai under whose purview alleged liturgical alterations were affirmed. These scholars question that the term "nozrim" pertained to Christians as the textual evidence in the Mishnah is lean at best. Additionally, scholars in this school view the "expulsion" of Christians from the synagogue as incidental—as John's Gospel suggests—and not usual, customary, nor widespread. Finally, those in this group view the "final separation" between Christians and the synagogue as gradual over a course of two centuries, mutual in that the two theologies radically differed, and more consensual among Jewish Christians who initiated the "break" from Judaism—and not the other way around.

We now turn our attention to the presumption that the Beth Din at Yavneh denied Scriptural status to the Christian writings, i.e., the Christian Gospels. This theory has support among both non-Christian and Christian scholars, e.g., George Foote Moore.

George Foote Moore, in his monumental work, *Judaism In the First Centuries of the Christian Era: The Age of Tannaim*, argues:

Before the death of Yohanan ben Zakkai, Gamaliel

II succeeded him, with the title *Nazi*, which Greek and Latin writers render "Patriarch," but for which we might use "President." His great endeavor was to secure the recognition of all Jewry for the Beth Din a Yavneh and submission to its authority. His colleagues thought him too arbitrary in asserting his own preeminence, and he was for a time deprived of the presidency of the academy (*yeshiva*). It was probably in his time that the long-standing strife between the schools of Shammai and Hillel was terminated by a general decision in favor of the latter, and the grave evil of conflicting observances, with the possibility of schism about them, overcome.

The controversy between the two schools over the question whether Ecclesiastes and the Song of Songs were Holy Scripture was decided by a majority vote in favor of both of them, following the opinion of the school of Hillel. Another decision in this period—the time and place are unknown—concerning what we call the canon of Scripture was that the Book of Ben Sira (Ecclesiasticus) was not sacred Scripture, nor any other books written from his time on. The passages in the Tosefta which report this decision name specifically "the gospel" (euangelion) and the books of the sectarians (or heretics), among which, in the context, it is fair to presume that Christian writings are at least included.[122]

Moore's Talmudic basis for his argument is found in Mishnah Yadaim 2:13 and Shabbat 13 (14): 5 to affirm his conclusion that Yavnean sages excluded the writings of the Christians (and ultimately Jewish Christians themselves from the synagogue).

However, Israeli scholar Gedaliah Alon, cites the fallacious nature of Moore's argument that "This view would lead to some very important historical conclusions, if it could be convincingly demonstrated [by historical evidence]."[123]

Alon argues that if the Sages during the time of Gamaliel II (100 CE) were compelled to decree that the Christian Gospels were not Holy Writ, then it logically follows that the Christian writings were widely distributed among the people, and had gained considerable acceptance "as at least as a sort of holy writings [sic]."[124]

This corollary, argues Alon, does not stand up to historical scrutiny, for while there were in the first century Jewish Christians within the larger Jewish community, one may presuppose the circulation of an Aramaic "gospel-text" but nothing in Hebrew. Additionally, Alon and other scholars view the New Testament as essentially anti-Semitic, for "it is not conceivable that a 'New Torah,' containing polemics against Judaism, and filled with events and legends dating back only two or three generations, should have been regarded by many Jews as a holy book." [125] The exception, urges Alon, would be the actual Jewish Christians themselves, and there is some doubt that they, at an early date, would regard their own written "evangel" as sacred writ.[126]

Moore, however, bases his theory upon exegetical data:

> The *gilyonim* and the books of the sectaries do not render the hands impure.[127]

> *Gilyonim* and books of the sectaries are not to be rescued (on the Sabbath) but are allowed to burn right where they are, along with the *'azkarot'* (Divine names that may be written on them).[128]

In rebuttal to Moore's theory, Alon comments:

> Those scholars who hold the (above) theory interpret the word 'gilyonim' to mean *'evangelyonim'* (the Gospels). Now it is true that the Babylonian Talmud mentions *"aven gilyon"*[129]

> Nevertheless, that is probably not the meaning in

the present context. In my opinion, the term refers to a "sheet" of writing material (parchment) such as is sewn to others of the kind to make a scroll. Basically, that is how the Talmud understands the word. That indeed is what Rabbi Judah makes explicit in his dissenting opinion.[130]

In his essay on the separation of Christianity from Judaism, R. Travers Herford writes that "Judaism was hardly at all affected by the rise and separation of Christianity, except while the process was going on."[131] The "process" covered about a period of fifty years, beginning "...with the ministry of Jesus and ending when the declaration against the *minim* (Jewish Christians) was officially made by the assembly of Rabbis at Yavneh, in the year 80 [CE] or thereabouts."[132] Jocz, *et al.*, suggest that the process of separation extended over a much longer period of time and the influence on Christianity of Judaism was considerable.[133]

Moore contends that Judaism was not only opposed to the adverse doctrinal Christian influence on the unity of God, "but to dualism of all kinds in the atmosphere of philosophical and religious thought."[134] The earlier efforts of Herford conclude that the synagogue's chief antagonists were Jewish Christians, that they "were the class of heretics most likely to be affected by regulations concerning the liturgy to be used in worship."[135] The previous quotation refers to Mishnah Megillah 4:8 where it is described how one may detect the presence of a *min* who would perturb Joshua b. Levi with questions concerning Scriptural exegesis.[136] On this Jocz observes that "the controversy between Judaism and Christianity was, to a large extent, exegetical in essence."[137] As observed above, Herford was convinced that the "minim" referenced in the Talmud were Jewish Christians.[138]

Martyn proposes the theory that the statements by John in his Gospel about the exclusion of Christians from the synagogue actually refer to an early form of the *Birkat ha-Minim*, or "the Blessing against the Heretics." This curse, writes Martyn, was officially institutionalized at Yavneh around 85-90 CE by Yohanan ben Zakkai to single out Christians.[139] This was part of a basic movement to close the ranks and to establish rabbinic orthodoxy after the destruction of the temple.[140]

The actual form of the Cairo Geniza *Birkat ha-Minim* that was discovered in 1949 in the Cairo Geniza text reads as follows:

> For the apostates let there be no hope. And let the arrogant government be speedily uprooted in our days. Let the *nozrim* and the *minim* be destroyed in a moment. And let them be blotted out of the Book of Life and not be inscribed together with the righteous. Blessed art thou, O Lord, who humbles the arrogant.[141]

Claudia Setzer observes that many scholars reason that the curse on the heretics described in rabbinic literature would naturally be understood as a reference to Christians. "A believer in Jesus who worshipped in a synagogue would be unable to repeat this prayer and pronounce a curse on himself." [142] Thus it would follow that the Christian worshipper would remove himself from the worship service, and is viewed by Martyn and others as a permanent exclusion. This reasoning views that John 9:22 is explicable as an instance of the use of *Birkat ha-Minim* to permanently expel Christians from Jewish worship. Sertzer argues, however, that this reconstruction of rabbinic literature rests on a number of assumptions.

First, either the term *nosrim* is original or *minim* would clearly designate Jews who believe in Jesus. Second, a Christian Jew in a synagogue would identify himself or herself as a heretic. Third, the *Birkat ha-Minim* was widely used in the Yavnean period. Fourth, the curse of *Birkat ha-Minim* carried with it the practice of expulsion from the synagogue. Fifth, the rabbis at Yavneh were engaged in "closing the ranks," and were increasingly exclusive and intolerant of divergent elements within the community. They had the power to implement a program of establishing uniform practice. Last, *Birkat ha-Minim* was used by other Jews as a means for ferreting out Christians who remained in the synagogue but did not openly proclaim faith in Jesus.[143]

However, as Sertzer and others have noted, recent challenges have focused on the ambiguity of the term *min*, the question of the originality and identity of the term *nosrim*, and issues surrounding the power and designated authority of the Yavnean sages.[144]

J.D. Cohen affirms Sertzer's conclusion that the broad application of *Birkat ha-Minim* to Christians no longer commands universal assent:

> Obviously the Christians of John's community were expelled from their local synagogues, but this hardly means that all Jews everywhere expelled Christians. Synagogues were not beholden to any central body; every community ran its synagogue in its own way. Even if the rabbis wished to expel Christians from all the synagogues of the empire, they lacked the power and the authority to do so. Furthermore, although by the fourth century the "benediction against heretics" was directed against Christians or some Jewish Christian sects, its original version was a generic denunciation of all heretics. The intent was not to single out Christians or any other specific group, but to proclaim the end of sectarianism.[145]

Cohen argues that one of the peculiar characteristics of the Mishnah was the prevalence of legal disputes between rabbis. As an example, the very first paragraph of the Mishnah opens with a question that receives three different answers, and virtually every page of rabbinic literature repeats this pattern with many variations.[146]

Legal disputes for the most part in second-temple literature were attributed to sects, and not to persons. As an example, the houses of Hillel and Shammai in pre-70 CE rabbinic literature were centers of disputes, but not among individuals. After 70 CE, the arguments between "houses" ceased and were replaced with disputations between masters. Despite the disputes, the individuals involved maintained normal social intercourse.

Cohen concludes:

> It is unlikely, therefore, that the rabbis felt a need to exclude anyone from their number; on the contrary, their ultimate success derived from the fact that they were prepared to absorb even those elements which originally opposed them. The real concession that the rabbis demanded of all comers was that they forgo any sectarian affiliation. Legal disputes would be tolerated, even fostered, but sectarian disputes must cease. This was the message of the benediction against heretics. The rabbis prayed that God destroy all those who persisted in maintaining a separatist identity in a world without a temple and in a society that was prepared to tolerate disputes.
>
> If this reconstruction is correct, the institution of the benediction against heretics was an important milestone in the self-definition of rabbinic Judaism, but not a crucial moment in the birth of Christianity. The separation of Christianity from Judaism was a process, not an event. The essential part of the process was that the church was becoming more and more gentile, and less and less Jewish, but the separation manifested itself in different ways in each local community where Jews and Christians dwelt together. In some places, the Jews expelled the Christians; in others, the Christians left of their own accord. The benediction against heretics perhaps shows why the Christians would have felt unwelcome in the rabbinic community of Palestine, but it has only minimal relevance to the process as a whole.[147]

However, one question remains: Did the motivation of the liturgical alteration — or the *Birkat ha-Minim* — lead to the outcome of a rabbinic concealment from the Jewish people of the true identity of Jesus as Messiah? Additionally, could not the aforementioned references in John's gospel, incidents that happened early in the ministry of Jesus, suggest a deliberate concealment by temple authorities that would continue with Yohanan ben Zakkai?

We now turn our attention to the actual textual evidence from the *Bavli* (*Babylonian Talmud*) and *Palestinian Recension* that relates to the *Birkat ha-Minim*:

1. For apostates (*mesummadim*) may there be no hope,
2. And the arrogant kingdom (*malkhut zadon*) uproot speedily in our days.
3. May the *nosrim* (Christians?) and the *minim* (heretics in general?) perish in an instant.
4. May they be blotted out of the book of the living, and may they not be written with the righteous (Ps 69:29).
5. Blessed art Thou, O Lord, who humbles the arrogant.[148]

Dunn observes that Bavli Berakhot 28a-29b is given as a *baraita* which claims to report events at Yavneh in the late first century CE, but notes that the baraita is found only in the Bavli.[149] In his analysis of Units 1 through 4 above, Dunn believes that the existence of *a Birkat Minim* can be traced back with some confidence to the first half of the second century CE, citing Justin's reference to the Jews cursing the Christians in synagogue.[150] What must be stressed, writes Dunn, is that the precise connection of the *Birkat ha-Minim* with editing synagogue liturgy at Yavneh is found only in late strata of Rabbinic literature, around the time of Gamaliel II and not an early date during the time of Yohanan ben Zakkai. Thus, this fact must be born in mind in reconstructing the history of the benediction, and too much weight should not be ascribed to the uncorroborated testimony of Bavli Berakhot 28b-29b.[151]

Though by modern technique it is impossible to reconstruct the original wording of the benediction from numerous variant texts, it is clear that all versions combine two quite disparate motifs. First, they pray for the downfall of the "arrogant kingdom" (i.e., Rome). Second, they pray for judgement on the *minim*, and the context, suggests Dunn, can only apply to Christians. Patristic evidence along with the previous quotation from the Palestinian recension indicates that the *noserim* was a reference to Christians.[152]

According to Bavli Berakhot 28b-29a, the *Birkat ha-Minim* was formulated at Yavneh, but it would be wrong to conclude that the rabbis had any authority to impose it upon any single synagogue in Palestine, or beyond into the Diaspora. Dunn notes that "the synagogue was not a Rabbinic institution and there was no mechanism by which the Rabbis could have imposed their will directly on it."[153]

Probably the single most difficult element contained in the argument is that of *textual dating*. Neusner observes that while we have no exact dates for the closure of any of the documents of Rabbinic literature — "all the dates we have are mere guesses" — we have solid grounds for the following:

> [1] Mishnah, [2] Tosefta, [3] Bavli for the exegetical writings on the Mishnah, and the three corresponding, and successive groups, Sifra and the two Sifres, levitical Rabbah, Pesiqta de Rab Kahana, Pesiqta Rabbati, then Ruth Rabbah, Esther Rabbah Part One, Lamentations Rabbah, and Song of Songs Rabbah — for the exegetical portions of Scripture.[154]

George Foote Moore argues that discussions of canonical writings at Yavneh were motivated by the Christian circulation of Christian books rather than arguments over other Jewish writings.[155] Wilson argues that Moore oversimplifies on this point, and notes that the canon was largely fixed before Yavneh, and there were many other heretical works to consider.[156] However, Wilson presents four arguments to support his thesis: First, recent consensus is dependent on two related perceptions: that post 70 CE Judaism was not monolithic nor was Christianity the sole challenge; that in post-70 Judaism previous studies, the variety and dissidence were underestimated and the threat from Christianity exaggerated. Second, philological arguments are often inconclusive, though critical, i.e., there is a consensus that *minim* means "heretic" in general, but "Christian heretic" is not indicative in the context.

Third, it is agreed almost without exception that the Christian works were included in the censured works by the rabbis.[157] Fourth, these teachings were intended to preserve the integrity of the Jewish community and not to attack the Christians. The argumentation was from a Jewish viewpoint and the intended audience was entirely Jewish.

> The Christian writings targeted could have come from Jewish or gentile Christian circles, and this brings us up against the familiar problem of dating. Are we dealing with first/second — or third/fourth century conflicts here? It is hard to tell, though Justin's evidence may just tip the balance in favor of the former.[158]

However, as previously observed, there is both uncertainty and sometimes confusion regarding dating the Mishnah.[159]

Neusner agrees with Wilson's observations, and notes that the corpus of Rabbinic literature spans the first seven centuries in the Common Era by sages who claimed to stand in the chain of tradition from Sinai "and uniquely possess the oral part of Torah, revealed by God to Moses at Sinai for oral formulation and oral transmission."[160]

This they possessed in addition to the written part of the Torah possessed by all Israel. Among the many, diverse documents produced by the Jews in the first seven centuries CE, only a small group is called, "Rabbinic literature." Three traits together suffice to distinguish Rabbinic literature from all other Jewish (ethnic) and Judaic (religious) writings of that age:

> [1] These writings of law and exegesis, revered as holy books, copiously cite the Hebrew Scriptures of ancient Israel ("written Torah");
>
> [2] They acknowledge the authority, and even the existence of no other Judaic (or gentile) books but only the ancient Israelite Scriptures.
>
> [3] These writings promiscuously and ubiquitously cite sayings attributed to named authorities, unique to those books themselves, most of them bearing the title "rabbi."[161]

Other Jewish monographs ordinarily qualify under the first plank of the Judaic definition, the same to be applied to Christian documents. The second plank, according to Neusner, would specifically exclude Christian writings. The third dismisses all writings of all Judaisms other than the dual Torah. Neusner comments:

> Other [Judaic] writings cite Scriptural heroes or refer to a particular authority; none except those of this Judaism sets forth, as does every Rabbinic document, extensive accounts of what a large number of diverse authorities say, let alone disputes among them "Rabbinic" is therefore an appropriate qualifier for this Judaism, since what distinguishes it from all other is the character of its authorities (the matter of title being a mere detail) and the myth that accounts for its distinctive character.[162]

According to Alon, the attitude of the Jewish sages towards Jewish Christians by the beginning of the second century is seen in the following from the Mishnah:

> Rabbi Eliezer was arrested by the Romans and charged with being a *Min*. They put him up on the

stand (*bamah*) to be tried. The *hegmon* (governor? Tribune?) said: 'how does an old man like you come to be involved in such matters?' The Rabbi answered: 'I put my faith in the Judge.' Of course, he meant his Father in Heaven, but the *hegmon* thought he was referring to him. So he said: 'Since you put your trust in me — *dimus* (dismissed)! You are discharged.' When Rabbi Eliezer left the stand he was upset because he had been arrested for *minut*. His disciples came to him to console him, but he would not be comforted. Then Rabbi Akiba entered and said: 'Rabbi, may I say something without giving offense?' He answered: 'Say on.' Said he: 'Is it possible that one of the *Minim* once told you something of their teaching that pleased you?' He answered: 'By heaven, you have reminded me! I was walking once along the main street of Sepphoris, and I met Jacob of Kefar Sikhnin, and he told me a bit of *minut* in the name of Yeshua ben Pantera, and I enjoyed it! That is why I was arrested for m*inut*, because I violated the Scripture that says, 'Remove thy way from her, and come not near the door of her house' (quoting Prov 5:6 as referring to a prostitute).[163]

The Tradition reveals a friendly exchange between the early Tannaim and some of the Jewish followers of Jesus — "but at the same time, the growing alienation between the two camps, approaching the proportions of a halakah forbidding discourse with *minim* in matters of Torah."[164]

Central to the historical context of *minim, nozrim*, and non-Rabbinic writings, would be a review of the rabbinic data in the Talmud that pertains to Jesus of Nazareth. When reviewing the Talmudic testimony concerning Jesus, the question arises: were the rabbis attempting to conceal his identity from non-Christian Jews, or are there other logical explanations based upon the evidence?

Talmudic Literature Pertaining to Jesus
During the Yavnean Age

References to Jesus are contained in both the Talmud and Midrash literature, yet many scholars agree that these references are legendary and lack historicity.[165] However, the Talmudic references provide some insight into the method and inclinations of the Yavnean sages who penned them two millennia ago. Klausner comments:

> They partake rather of the nature of vituperation and polemic against the founder of a hated party, than objective accounts of historical value.[166]

In his examination of the data, Laible observes:

> Two points are continually presented to us in a striking way: First, the extraordinary paucity and scantiness of those accounts; second, their fabulous character.[167]

From an historical viewpoint, Jocz describes this as "curious and disappointing..." for "we should have expected historically well authenticated evidence from Jewish sources respecting the person of Jesus of Nazareth. But this is not so."[168] Klausner suggests two reasons contribute to the glaring omission of information. First, the sages of the Second Temple era rarely alluded to historical events in general; second, the turbulent times of the Herods and Roman procurators overshadowed the person and ministry of Jesus. When, in time, Christianity became a competing religion with Judaism, the rabbis possessed little or no information of the facts.[169] This may be the best explanation, yet difficult to understand how the sages at Yavneh could have totally ignored the available information from other sources.

The rabbinic literature, in contrast to the historical evidence from Greek, Roman, and Gnostic writers presented above, may be a "negative version of Josephus' twofold description,"[170] to accuse Jesus of sorcery and to lead the people astray:

> On the eve of Passover they hung Jeshu. And the crier went forth before him forty days, saying, "He goes forth to be stoned because he has practiced magic and deceived and led Israel astray. Anyone who knows anything in his favor let him come and declare concerning him." And they found nothing in his favor. And they hung him on the eve of Passover.[171]

> And a teacher has said, "Jesus the Nazarene practiced magic and led astray and deceived Israel.[172]

> It is tradition that Rabbi Eliezer said to the sages, "Did not Ben Stada bring spells from Egypt in a cut which was upon his flesh?" They said to him, "He was a fool, and they do not base a proof upon a fool." Ben Stada is Ben Pandira.[173]

The first passage is the clearest reference of rabbinic tradition, and for that reason is deleted in some manuscripts.[174] Jocz observes that the Talmud seems to adopt two methods in dealing with opposing parties. The first is to ridicule, and the other is to ignore any adversary altogether. The Talmud adopted the first in its presentation of the life of Jesus, and the second in its attitude toward John the Baptist.[175] Klausner analyzes another important event in Jewish history that finds no space in the Talmud. Klausner observes that had it not been for 1 and 2 Maccabees and the writings of Josephus, the Talmud would not have communicated to all generations the very name of Judas Maccabaeus. However, under "strained controversy," as Jocz writes, "the Talmud makes some statements about the person of Jesus."[176] Still, later additions in rabbinic literature stood in direct reaction against "Christian oppression," that was "a highly treasured, private form of vengeance in return for the attitude of the Christians towards the Jews."[177]

In the Mishnah, there is one clear extant reference to

Jesus, generally held to be the oldest one pertaining to Jesus.[178] Rabbi Simeon b. Azzasi said:

> I found a family register in Jerusalem, and in it was written, "Such a one is a bastard through (a transgression of the law of) thy neighbors wife", confirming the words of Joshua.[179]

Jocz notes that there are also several baraitas and a number of *Midrashic* allusions either to Jesus himself of the disciples of Jesus. Jocz comments:

> Only occasionally does the actual name of Jesus occur, in the form of *Yeshu, Yeshu ha-nozri* (or, *nozri*) or *Yeshu ben Panteri* (also *Pantera, Pandera*).[180]

It is more often in the literature that Jesus is referred to as *ish ploni* ("the anonymous one") or *oto ha-ish* ("that man"), some scholars attribute to medieval censorship.[181] Jocz observes that later Jewish sages seem to have confused Jesus with Ben Stada, noted above, thereby adding another synonym to the collection.[182]

Laible, Strack, Herford, and Klausner have carefully examined the Talmudic references to Jesus, and their detailed discussion may be pursued by the reader for more detail.[183] For our purpose here, the Talmudic portrait of Jesus appears to be based upon hearsay evidence:

> Jesus, called *ha-Notzri, B. Stada,* or *Pandira,* was born out of wedlock.[184] His mother was called Miriam, and was a dresser of women's hair.[185] Her husband was *Pappus b. Judah,* and her paramour *Pandira.* She is said to have been the descendant of princes and rulers, and to have played the harlot with a carpenter.[186] Jesus had been in Egypt, and had brought magic thence. He was a magician, and deceived and led astray Israel.[187] He sinned and caused the multitude to sin.[188] He mocked at the words of the wise, and was excommunicated.[189]

He was tainted with heresy.[190] He called himself

God, also the Son of man, and said that he would go up to heaven.[191] He made himself live by the name of God.[192] He was tried in Lydda (Lud) as a deceiver and as a teacher of apostasy; witnesses were concealed so as to hear his statements, and a lamp was lighted over him that his face might be seen.[193] He was executed in Lydda, on the eve of Passover, which was also the eve of Sabbath; he was stoned and hung, or crucified. A herald proclaimed, during forty days, that he was to be stoned, and invited evidence in his favor, but none was given.[194] He (the name "Balaam" is ascribed to him in the literature) was put to death by Pinhas the Robber (Pontius Pilatus), and at the time was thirty-three years old, having been punished in Gehenna by means of boiling filth.[195] He was "near to the kingdom", had five disciples, and under the name of "Balaam" was excluded from the world to come.[196]

Jocz observes that two things are apparent in the Talmudic account: First, the rabbis deliberately attempted to contradict events recorded in the Gospels; second an effort was made to present Jesus in an unfavorable light.[197] Hennecke concludes:

On the whole one is forced to admit that in the Talmud Jesus is nothing else than the reflection of Jewish—or Gentile—Christian portrait of Christ, *but naturally distorted by Jewish aversion.*[198]

Stephen G. Wilson argues that rather than aversion or concealment, the nature and scope of the rabbinic literature in the age of Tannaim had entirely different motivations:

Even on the most optimistic count, allusions to Jesus and his followers make up only a miniscule portion of the voluminous rabbinic tradition. True, censorship may account for the deletion of some material, but this would not change the balance significantly. It is commonly thought that the paucity of rabbinic evidence shows that Jews were largely unconcerned about Christians in the earlier centuries. This may be a false assumption. What the rabbis put into their writings was not the sum total of their views on all matters, but rather a range of opinion on a selection of narrowly defined issues. Moreover, in the first two centuries CE most Jews probably were not "rabbinic," in the sense that they were ruled by some central rabbinic authority, so that even if it is thought that the rabbis gave little thought to Christianity, it does not follow that other Jews did the same.[199]

Wilson further argues that the Jewish reaction to Christianity in Jewish sources is that Jesus was perceived as a heretic and outcast, along with a magician and deceiver of the people in particular.[200] Oral accounts of his birth were ridiculed, and the reputation of both Jesus and his mother was besmirched.

Two theological concepts were undermined, Wilson observes. First, the idea of the Divine becoming human; and second, the notion of the division of the Divine unity in a "two powers" debate.[201] In addition, rabbis no doubt still recalled the earlier flight from Jerusalem of Christians to escape the onslaught of Roman domination in 70 CE, which left Jewish resistance depleted, and ultimately resulted in the mass murder of a million or more Jews at the hands of the Romans. Further, toward the end of the Yavnean age, the Bar Cochba rebellion in 132 CE caused additional strains on Jewish and Christian relations.[202]

Ancient Israel had been commanded by God to build a holy temple as a dwelling place for the "Name" of God [203] and through all generations the prophets reminded the people of the "glorious temple where our fathers praised [G-d]." [204]

Though there were always theological and practical differences between Jews, all Jews contemplated their relationship with God in connection with the temple.[205]

It was the temple that "stood as the nexus between man and God."[206]

Herod's beautification project of rebuilding the temple would encompass an entire generation, and though condemned by the Essenes, the Pharisees taught that the temple sacrifices were the true way to please God and to reconcile the sinner to God.[207]

Both traditional Jews and Christian Jews viewed the destruction of the temple in 70 CE with contrasting attitudes. Christians remembered the words of their Lord and forsook the city many months, even years, before the conflagration.[208] The Jewish people themselves admitted the sins and failings of Jerusalem, and the Lord's visitation in judgment.[209] With the holy temple destroyed, and the great city in ashes, Jews scattered abroad. Some fled to Caesarea, others to Galilee in the rural regions. The Roman government replaced the temple tax imposed by the Pharisees with their own *Fiscus Judaicus*, a forced payment to the Olympian god Jupiter.[210]

On the eve of the destruction, Yohanan ben Zakkai, the supreme "Rabban" of Jerusalem, boldly had himself smuggled out of Jerusalem in a coffin to General Vespasian's camp. Because there are three written accounts of the same events in the Tradition, historians can only attempt to put pieces of the puzzle together.

Some scholars believe Yohanan negotiated for the city of Yavneh, to be allowed Roman escort to that port city with his disciples, in order to begin an academy. Other scholars believe Yohanan was compelled to go to Yavneh by Vespasian under Roman guard where Yavneh would serve as a post-war detention center. The historical account, in this writer's view, does not suggest one version over another.[211] What is central, however, is that Yohanan pleaded for—and was granted—Yavneh where, in fact, he established an academy for Torah study that would reformulate Judaism.

What Rome had attempted to destroy physically, the heart of Torah, could not be taken from the heart of the Jew. The commandments of God given at Sinai, and the covenant relationships could not be destroyed. Torah study could not be destroyed which from birth was burned into the soul of every Jewish child. Even after the embers of the city had cooled in 70 CE, the precious synagogue remained intact in distant locations, and the cherished memories that every Jew carried in his heart of the glorious days of the Monarchy gave him a sense of identity and purpose. During the Herodian period, the anticipation of *Messiah*, who would be a superhuman sent by God to vindicate Israel before all her enemies, would fill the Jewish apocalyptic imagination, when the Roman beast would be slain at last.[212]

Could the people of Jerusalem see a strong individual such as Yohanan ben Zakkai as a messianic figure? The historical records provide no answers. But Yohanan's strong, yet peace-loving countenance, provided the impetus for his natural leadership, first among the Sanhedrin in Jerusalem, and later as president of the Beth Din at Yavneh.[213]

Yohanan's master was none other than the great Hillel, whose moral and ethical teachings mirrored those of Jesus. Some scholars believe Yohanan and Jesus knew one another, that the "Zacchaeus" mentioned in the Gospels was none other than Yohanan ben Zakkai, who may have been about the same age as Jesus.[214]

The temple's destruction clearly doomed a national Jewish state, and the spiritual essence of Israel had to be redefined, both for Jews in the land and those in the Diaspora. From about 70 to 85 CE, Yohanan led this redevelopment with former Pharisees who would now be "sages."[215] Unlike the Sanhedrin in Jerusalem that wielded political authority and constrained autonomy under Roman procurators, the sages at Yavneh were tenuous leaders who had little trust from the people, and would not have true "rabbinic" authority until well into the fourth century.[216]

Conzelmann, Neusner, *et al.*, have well described the constraints by the Romans of Jews under their laws,[217] while Schurer, Vermes and Millar have traced the significant impact of Jewish resettlements through the Diaspora.[218]

The question as to Yohanan's authority at Yavneh, and whether he supervised a policy of exclusion towards Jewish Christians, relates to his function as *Nasi*, not to his title as *Rabban*.[219] The documented binding enactments at Yavneh under Yohanan must be seen in light of the fact that the High Court was stripped of all judicial autonomy, that binding policies had to do with matters of faith.[220] The tradition reveals that Yohanan desired among all things to preserve Torah study for all time, to keep temple ritual alive through the Feast of Tabernacles, and to preserve the continuity of Jewish expression.[221] The question is, did the new "Nazarene" movement pose a real threat to historical Judaism?

The known ordinances and enactments of Yohanan that are recorded in the Mishnah, are divided into three groups. First, the priestly offerings and privileges; second, the celebration of the New Moon and festivals, dates; and third, the disposition of the emoluments of the fallen temple, and the proselyte's offering and fourth-year fruits.[222] In all, Yohanan enacted nine ordinances that were strictly *liturgical* in scope.[223] Scholars agree that it would be unreasonable to assume that these were not the only ones instituted by the High Court. However, what information we do have regarding Yohanan ben Zakkai is ascertainable only because of later additions to the Mishnah.[224] Regarding the dating of much of the Mishna material, again we are often left to historical guesswork.[225]

Thus, in the literary context of the Age of Tannaim, particularly the Yavnean period of about 70-135 CE, is it conceivable that the sages could have concealed the true identity of Jesus (as Messiah) from the Jewish people? Two variant schools have been examined. The first group of scholars, i.e., Schurer, Jocz, George Foote Moore, Sigal, Parkes, Alon, Herford, *et al.*, argue that the "writings of the heretics" condemned at Yavneh were the Christian Gospels that were already in circulation. The *Birkat ha-Minim* malediction, they argue, occurred early in John's Gospel (9:22) and was fully codified at Yavneh in about 80 CE under Yohanan ben Zakkai. The *Nozrim* mentioned in rabbinic literature referred to Christians, and that the expulsion of the Christians from the synagogue was an early phenomenon, beginning at the time where the Gospels were written.

The second group of scholars, best represented by Neusner, Cohen, Kimmelman, Hornbury, Wilson, Dun, Setzer, et al., purport that the "writings of the heretics" involved non-Jewish writings, and that the historical evidence that the Christian Gospels were included is weak. The Christians would have not had a formal corpus, or "Torah" in written form early in the Yavnean period. These scholars view the *birkat ha-minim* as a pronouncement against all heretics in general, and may have included Christians in particular. The textual accounts in the Mishnah, they argue, are later additions and incomplete.

Additionally, the date for the "Eighteen Benedictions" emendation better suggests a much later time of Gamaliel II, who succeeded Yohanan ben Zakkai, and not Yohanan as the chief architect. These scholars question *nozrim* as pertaining to Christians for lack of textual evidence. Further, the "expulsion" of Christians from the synagogue in John's gospel was indicative of incidents—and not conclusive of a widespread phenomenon that occurred in the majority of synagogues. In fact, they conclude, the separation of the two religions, Judaism and Christianity, was a gradual evolution, and not climactic through a single, or series of events.

Rabban Yohanan ben Zakkai and his disciples analyzed the destruction of Jerusalem and its holy temple in light of Torah study, particularly in the context of Hosea 6:6: "It is love that I desire, and not sacrifice." Jews would suspend temple sacrifices in lieu of sacrificial deeds of love and prayers. The *abodah* or "prayer worship", was no longer supplemental temple worship,[226] it was now the essence of worship.[227] For this reason, Yohanan set a course of liturgical development, with all other matters secondary. While the Beth Din at Yavneh attempted to assert authority over calendar issues,[226] there were socially powerful elements that resisted rabbinic claims to authority down through the fourth century. With the proliferation of non-Jewish historical accounts that bore witness to Jesus of Nazareth, and the existence of Gospel accounts by the end of the first century, it is unlikely that the tenuous rabbinic leadership at Yavneh could have succeeded in concealing Jesus' person, life, and message from Jewish people throughout Palestine in particular, and the greater Roman Empire in general.[227]

In the last quarter of the first century, two groups of individuals posed a threat to historical Judaism from the outside that gave impetus for Yohanan ben Zakkai to lead the reformulation of Judaism. First, from the rabbinic viewpoint, the presence of false messiahs caused both confusion among the people and a strong negative reaction from Roman authorities who, in the process of suppressing many of these "messiahs", killed or displaced many innocent Jews in the process.[228] The most acclaimed false messiah, in the minds of most sages, was Jesus of Nazareth. Others included Theudas (44 CE),[229] Judas of Galilee, founder of the Zealots,[230] Benjamin the Egyptian (59 CE),[231] Menachem Son of Judas of Galilee (66 CE),[232] and "the flaming prophet" who died during the destruction of Jerusalem in 70 CE in an attempt to rally Jews to protect the temple.[233]

Each of these "messiahs" was self-delusional and ultimately destroyed themselves through selfish ambition. The messianic expectation among the rabbis and people was far removed from a carpenter's death on a Roman cross, or the maniacal exploits of false messiahs.[234] The second group that threatened Judaism was the existence of Jewish Christian sects that are often alluded to in the New Testament. Ebionites A observed all of the Torah commandments, followed Pharisaic Judaism and believed in the traditional Hebrew Scriptures. They rejected Pauline doctrine regarding Jesus as a sinner, but accepted Jesus as both prophet and Messiah though denying his virgin birth and divinity.[235] Ebionites B were Jewish Christians who joined with Gentile Christians and developed a God-Messiah concept surrounding

Jesus. They observed both the Jewish Sabbath and the Lord's Day (*Sunday*).[236] The Nazarenes accepted Christological theology carte blanch, that Jesus was Son of God, born of a Virgin and the Holy Spirit, and accepted the epistles of Paul. They stood in stark contrast to the Jewish sages—"the Scribes and the Pharisees."

Jerome was no less vitriolic towards the sages in his *Homilia*.[237] Jewish [Christian] Gnostics adhered to the laws of the Torah, believed in Jesus as Messiah, or prophet, as superhuman with attributes of Divine power. Their Gnostic tendencies were expressed in the view that the Messiah was an embodiment of a primordial spiritual force which had originally resided in Adam, was passed to the Patriarchs, and was finally made manifest in Jesus. They also expressed a Greek notion through the exaltation of earth, air, water and fire, and a dualism in that the universe consists of two opposing principles, namely, good and evil juxtaposed in eternal conflict.[238]

The Elkesaites are believed to have begun as a Jewish Christian sect by Elkesai, who "appeared" in Transjordan east of the Dead Sea in the third year of Trajan's reign, or the year 100 CE. He preached the Jewish way of life and proclaimed himself to be a prophet, urging his followers to face Jerusalem when they pray.[239] Alon rightly asked what prompted the Yavnean sages to place Jewish Christianity outside the Jewish fold? They would eventually regard Elkesaites as worse than Christians who had never been Jews.[240]

Direct contacts between rabbis and Christians during the Yavnean period were few, thus the polemical overtones in rabbinic literature are not high. Bavli Sanhedrin 107b may be typical, but does not reflect the tone of the *Toledot Yeshu* of the fifth century, long after Yavneh. The Christian doctrine of the atonement would later be addressed in the fourth century, but the historical evidence from the Talmud suggests that Yavnean sages had a scant knowledge of Christian teachings.[241] Christianity was perceived by rabbis in the first century as both a marginal and radical movement. This new "Nazarene" movement at first had a greater impact upon the Jewish community in general, but by the beginning of the second century, essentially because of the travels and teachings of Paul and other Christians, it was largely gentile.[242]

During the Yavnean period, ca. 70-135 CE, Jewish believers in Jesus produced a theological corpus known as the New Testament. While the Christian writings were circulating throughout the Roman Empire individually, for the first one hundred years the Christians' only revealed Scripture was the same Torah that all Israel had received as teaching from God. As far as the evidence indicates, these same people appealed to the Torah to validate their faith and studied the Torah to explain it.[243] Jewish disciples and apostles set forth in the pages of the New Testament a Judaism that stood on equal ground with historic Judaism, a Judaism that found fulfillment in Jesus of Nazareth.

Though John's Gospel has been often criticized as anti-Semitic and condemning "the Jews" for the crucifixion, John was a loyal Israelite and adhered to Torah. Chilton and Neusner observe:

> While later on a shift in category-formation distinguished between Judaism and Christianity, even here Christianity insisted on its patrimony and inheritance out of ancient Israel. Not only so, but Christianity would represent itself for all time as the sole valid continuation of the faith and worship of ancient Israel. That is to say, Christianity portrayed itself as (other) Judaisms ordinarily portrayed themselves, and out of precisely the same shared Torah at that.

> Consequently, to distinguish between the religious world of the New Testament and an alien Judaism denies the authors of the New Testament books their most fiercely held claim and renders incomprehensible much that they said. Whether Jesus, insisting on his Judaic conception of God's kingdom, or Paul, explaining how in his Judaic conception of Israel through Christ gentiles enter (are "grafted into") Israel, whether the Evangelists, linking Jesus

> to the house of David and much that he said and
> did to Israelite prophecy, or the author of the Letter
> to the Hebrews recasting the entire history of Israel
> from an account of salvation to one of sanctifica-
> tion—the picture is uniform. But then how can we
> grasp the New Testament's Judaism if we do not
> treat its religion as a Judaism?[244]

Thus, the New Testament was born out of the Yavnean period, not as a foreign body of literature, but as a legitimate formulation of Judaism on equal footing with the sages and all other expressions of Judaism. All of the Judaisms insisted on their unique truth system based on Torah study, and the New Testament should be treated in light of its principal subject who declared himself as the one who (literally) "filled up full" the Old Testament Law.

The conclusion of many recent researchers challenges the following earlier presuppositions about the *Birkat ha-Minim*: First, the term *minim* clearly designated Christian Jews who believed in Jesus. Second, Christian Jews in synagogues would identify themselves as heretics in refusing to recite the benediction against heretics. Third, the *Birkat ha-Minim* was in wide circulation during the Yavnean period. Fourth, the Yavnean rabbis were intolerant of all "other" Judaisms and were seeing a uniformity of liturgy and theology. Fifth, the *Birkat ha-Minim* curse presupposed automatic expulsion from the synagogue. Last, the *Birkat ha-Minim* was a litmus test used by non-Christian Jews to discover Christian Jews who remained in the synagogue without revealing their faith in Jesus.[245]

However, this reconstruction has been recently questioned, for the term *min* is ambiguous, along with the term *nosrim*, and the issue of authority and power of the Yavnean sages.[246] The "closing of the ranks" by the rabbis at Yavneh around 85-90 CE, as Martyn suggests, is largely drawn from a form of the *Birkat ha-Minim* discovered in a text in the Cairo Geniza that reads as follows:

For the apostates let there be no hope. And let the arrogant government be speedily uprooted in our days. Let the *nosrim* and the *minim* be destroyed in a moment. And let them be blotted out of the Book of Life and not be inscribed together with the righteous. Blessed art thou, O Lord, who humbles the arrogant.[247]

Setzer observes that the rabbinic reference attributes it to Samuel the Small at Yavneh and implies that anyone who falters in repeating it would be removed.[248] In around 150 CE, Justin complained that Jews both cursed Christ and Christians in their synagogues.[249] There is historical evidence to suggest that there was a "blessing" against the *minim* in the late first century. I question any connection between the blessing and the expulsion of Christians from the synagogue, and any deliberate attempt by the rabbis to conceal the identity of Jesus of Nazareth from the Jewish people.

Summary

Therefore, the following conclusions are within logical reach based upon the current available historical information:

First, there was no precedent for the *Birkat ha-Minim* in the synagogue of the first century other than local exclusionary actions by some synagogues.[250]

Second, the benediction may have been composed at an early date, but there is no evidence that it was implemented during the time of Yohanan ben Zakkai. Instead, it was probably formally implemented under Gamaliel II in the first quarter of the second century.[251]

Third, the benediction did not contain the word *nozrim*, but only the word *minim,* and was directed mainly against Jewish Christians. Schwaab believes that the second benediction was also directed against Christians.[252]

Fourth, the theological differences between historic Judaism and Christian Jews began early in the Gospel narratives with the inauguration of Jesus' ministry, was perpetuated by pre-70 CE Pharisaic sectarianism.

Fifth, the evidence from the Mishnah seems to suggest that Yohanan ben Zakkai was a strong pacifist, and collaborated with the Romans in order to secure peace for Israel.[253]

The accumulation of oral traditions concerning Jesus, along with the presence of at least the Gospel portion of the New Testament, and the tenuous nature of the rabbinic authority at Yavneh, indicates strong doubt that the rabbis could have concealed Jesus' ministry and message from the Jewish people. That the infant church was primarily Jewish well beyond the Yavnean period into the second century, provides evidence that the message of Jesus the Messiah was transcending the prejudicial writings of some sages.

What the nature and scope of the Mishnah testimony about Jesus reveals is ridicule towards the historical Jesus based upon hearsay evidence. Jesus is portrayed as a "magician" and a "sorcerer", and major historical accounts such as Josephus, other Greek and even Gnostic accounts, along with oral and written accounts that comprised the New Testament provides a more balanced portrait of Jesus of Nazareth.

Thus, I view the major portions of the Mishnah pertaining to Jesus are essentially legendary and prejudicial which is consistent with the New Testament presentation of some of the religious leaders that opposed Jesus early in his ministry. Thus, while Yavneh reformulated Judaism and redefined its theology and the significance of the destruction of the temple, the Academy at Yavneh paved the way for the eventual "parting of the ways" between Judaism and Christianity.

Epilogue: Yohanan ben Zakkai
A Leader For All Time

THE PROPHET OF OLD had spoken the oracle of God: "I desire mercy, and not sacrifice, and acknowledgement of God rather than burnt offerings" (Hosea 6:6). Through the ages, the Holy Scriptures had chronicled habitual idolatry through which Israel had forsaken her Lord to serve foreign deities. The Lord had said that Jerusalem would be his "dwelling place forever" (Jer 17:25), but in 586 BCE, the Babylonians showed no mercy as they breached the walls of the Great City and destroyed the holy temple.

By the rivers of Babylon, the exiled psalmist wept bitter tears with his people as he remembered Zion. In utter humiliation, the Jews could not sing the songs of the Lord, so in despair they hung their harps on poplar branches. Their cruel captors, with scorn and derision, demanded that they sing "songs of joy." The psalmist inquired, "How can we sing the songs of [Adonai] while in a foreign land?" (Psalm 137).

The psalmist answered his own inquiry with words that would live through all generations, and much later with Yohanan as he gazed upon the second temple destruction: "If I forget you, O Jerusalem, may my right hand forget its skill. May my tongue cling to the roof of its mouth if I do not remember you, if I do not consider Jerusalem [to be] my highest joy" (Psalm 137:5-6).

With the temple in ruins and the great city in ashes, Yohanan ben Zakkai set his heart and mind to remember Jerusalem and the temple of her Lord forever. Christian Jews, remembering the words of their Lord, had fled to

Pella before the Roman siege. The Romans had murdered most of the Sadducees and the few that survived fled into the surrounding countryside. Tens of thousands of Yohanan's countrymen were dead, their bodies strewn throughout the city streets. Mirroring the concentration camps of the twentieth century, in some areas of Jerusalem corpses were stacked as high as eight feet. Vespasian gave Yohanan and his former Pharisees the city of Yavneh as a refuge, and whether they were forced there as detainees or "rewarded" the coastal town by the new emperor, we can only conjecture from the records.

Upon arriving at Yavneh, Yohanan and his disciples pondered the destruction of the sacred temple. They asked one another, "How could God forsake his own temple and allow its destruction?" For the sins of "this generation" God would bring a second destruction of his own temple and a second captivity, only this time it would be a Diaspora from which Israel would not recover its national identity until the mid-twentieth century.

At Yavneh Yohannan and his disciples considered the desecration of the temple by Antiochus a century and a half before, and its historical significance for Jews through all time. Unlike the Babylonian captivity, the courageous Maccabee family gave Yohanan inspiration for his vision at Yavneh in the ashes of the second temple destruction. The story of the Maccabees is the most familiar story explained to every Jewish child from antiquity to the present:

The Roman historian Josephus, records the death of Ptolemy Epiphanes of Egypt and the son who succeeded him, Ptolemy Philometor who was young and powerless. Antiochus Epiphanes of Syria invaded Egypt with a large force and took Memphis. But before he could besiege Alexandria, the Romans ordered him to leave Egypt. Fearing the power of Rome, he traveled back through Judea to Syria.

During this time, Jerusalem was in chaos, for Onias the High Priest had died, and his brothers, Jason and Menelaus, fought for the high priesthood. When Jason defeated his brother, Menelaus and his followers defected to Antiochus to offer their services as scouts for the invasion of Judea. Friends of Menelaus inside the city opened the gates, and as a result, Antiochus marched on Jerusalem and took it with little resistance. Many in the opposition party were killed, whereupon Antiochus ransacked the city and returned to Syria.

Two years later, in 167 BCE, Antiochus came back to Jerusalem with his entire army. Again, traitors gave him safe passage into the city. Once inside, he slaughtered the inhabitants and murdered even those who provided him safe passage. He dismantled the city walls, set fire to the wealthiest parts of the city, and stationed a Macedonian garrison high in a citadel that overlooked the temple. He then carried away the vast wealth of the temple — golden vessels and indescribable treasures — and put an end to all temple sacrifices. He knew that the Law of Moses condemned such actions, yet he blasphemed the sacred altar by offering a swine on it, compelled all Jews to forsake their worship of God and forbade the circumcision of their children. Those who refused to cooperate were mutilated, strangled, or crucified, with their dead children hung from their necks.

From a safe distance the Samaritans learned of the Jewish suffering under Antiochus, and they dispatched a courier with a letter to Antiochus that denied any Jewish relationship. In a hateful action that would live forever in the minds of Jews, the Samaritans asked that their "temple without a name" on Mt. Gerizim be known as "Zeus Hellenios" (see John 4:22).

At about this time, in the small village of Modin there was a Jewish priest named Mattathias who had five sons: John, Simon, Judas (called Maccabeus), Eleazar, and Jonathan. Antiochus sent soldiers to Modin to compel the Jews to sacrifice blasphemously as he had previously ordered other Jews. The Syrians, aware that Mattathias was the city leader, went to him knowing that his "first sacrifice" would persuade the people to follow in like manner. But Mattathias refused, and declared that even if all of the people obeyed Antiochus' commands, he and his sons would rather suffer death than to commit such a blasphemy.

However, to the horror of all Jews present, an unknown Jew stepped forward and performed the sacrifice as Antiochus had required. Outraged, Mattathias and his five sons unsheathed their broad-blade knives and immediately dispatched the man. A fight ensued, and the brothers managed to kill the king's officer and his soldiers, and overturned the pagan altar. Mattathias cried out to the people that "whoever is zealous for the laws of his country and the worship of God, then follow me."

The bold priest and his five sons fled to the desert, and many others followed with their wives and children where they lived like Bedouin in the hills and caves. The Syrians were swift on their trail, and pursued many of them to their caves where they were cornered. The Jews would not block the openings of the caves and did not resist their tormentors when the cave openings were set ablaze. About a thousand rebels died. Mattathias, now the appointed leader by the people, along with many followers was able to escape unharmed. Mattathias now directed the people to fight on the Sabbath lest they all suffer death; the large army destroyed the pagan altars and then killed those who had sacrificed upon them. The Jewish male children were then ordered circumcised in obedience to their Lord.

Mattathias, however, became ill at about a year into his command, and advised his sons to continue the courageous struggle for freedom. He also told them to select his son Simon as paternal adviser, and because of his courage and strength, to select Maccabeus (Judas) as the army commander.

After the death of his father in 167 BCE, along with his brothers and followers, Judas Maccabeus drove the Syrians completely from the land. The Samaritan governor, Apollonius, advanced his army against Judas, but was quickly defeated and killed. After that, the governor of Coele-Syria, was totally destroyed, even tough his army vastly outnumbered Judas'.

Meanwhile, at the direction of the Syrians, the Greek

general Ptolemy led yet a third army against Judas consisting of forty thousand infantry and seven thousand cavalry. Undaunted, Judas assembled his men and urged them to "be bold and to put their trust in God." He then dismissed all of the newly married men and new property owners to go home. But he realized that he had only three-thousand men left who were poorly armed.

Ptolemy encamped at Emmaus where he planned a surprise night attack. Using Jewish traitors as scouts and guides, he sent Gorgias with six thousand troops to prosecute the attack. However, Judas already knew of the plan, and decided to counter attack at Ptolemy's weakest point, that is, at the point when they were divided. Judas' men left many fires burning in their camp as they set out on an all-night march to Emmaus. When Gorgias discovered the abandoned Jewish camp, he pursued the enemy into the mountains.

Meanwhile as dawn approached, Judas reached Emmaus, attacked the sleeping Syrians and killed three thousand soldiers, then pursued the enemy into the hills. Judas returned to the enemy camp where he took all the weapons and supplies. When Gorgias and his men saw from a distance that their camp was destroyed, they fled in fear.

Lysias, who had been left in charge in Syria while Antiochus was in Persia, now invaded Judea with sixty thousand infantry and five thousand cavalry and camped at Bethsura. Judas confronted Lysias' vast army with only ten thousand men, but was able to kill about five thousand. Lysias was disturbed to see the desperate demeanor of the Jews, so he immediately called back his troops and returned to Antioch, where he made preparations to increase his army and supplies for yet another invasion.

Judas then declared to the people that God had given his people these many victories, and that they should march to Jerusalem to purify the temple and to offer sacrifices in honor to God. When they arrived in the city, Judas ordered some of the soldiers to continue fighting Syrian troops who were barricaded in the citadel. At the same time, Judas and the rest of the men purified the temple, which was laid waste with weeds growing inside the sanctuary. They rebuilt the altar, restored the sacred implements, rekindled the lamp stand, and burned incense. Three long years to the day had passed since Antiochus had blasphemed the temple. Judas and his men celebrated with a great feast that lasted eight days, that would come to be known as the Festival of Lights.

The meaning of Hanukkah in history has less to do with the cleansing of the temple than with the miracle that occurred in the sanctuary. For when the rebels first entered the sanctuary, there was enough oil left to fuel the altar candles for two days. But the miracle they witnessed was that the light of those candles stayed strong and bright for *eight* days.

In just over two hundred years later, a great Roman army again besieged Jerusalem and the sacred sanctuary was again laid waste. Through the ashes and countless bodies that lined the city streets arose a great Jewish leader of integrity and peace, Yohanan ben Zakkai, who lived to build a great Academy at Yavneh, in which he and his disciples would devote themselves to Torah study and the reformulation of ancient Judaism. For Yohanan, Torah study was the *light* that would burn in the heart of all Jews.

"Monsters under the bed"

We began this study with a theory among some "popular" Evangelical writers that early Jewish sages at Yavneh, deliberately concealed the identity of Jesus as the true Messiah from the Jewish people. Additionally, that Yohanan ben Zakkai and his disciples excluded Christians (the *Birkat ha-Minim*), and banned their writings ("writings of the heretics"). However, after careful examination of the records available to us, in my view, this theory has no historical support. On the contrary, the historical record reveals a bold individual of moral character who placed the best interests of his people Israel before his own.

Evidence suggests that the Gospels and other New Testament letters were widely circulated and read late in the first century, contrary to the opinion of some scholars who will not admit their early existence as it would lend support to an accepted Christian "Torah" existing among believers. However, the person and message of Jesus of Nazareth was not only well attested by the New Testament documents, but by many other non-Christian sources, as well. This indeed is a topic for another study altogether.

Still, questions remain: What was the purpose of the condemnation of the heretics and why did the Talmudic testimony of Jesus portray such a low view of him? In my view, there were a number of reasons for the heightened tensions between the two Judiasms:

First, the condemnation of the heretics widened the breach between historic Judaism and the new Judaism of Jewish Christians. The message of Jesus as presented in the New Testament was clearly in contrast to historic Judaism—a "new wine," said Jesus, to burst the old wine skins of the temple Pharisees. Jesus was marginalized by the established temple system as he proclaimed an inclusiveness by accepting "sinners" and gentiles as part of God's greater kingdom.

Second, the New Testament writings and the apostolic "evangelism" also contributed to the widening rift; historic Judaism was not "evangelistic" by nature. The Gospels viewed the Law as a means by God to lead the sinner to faith in Jesus.

Third, Judaism viewed the Law as supreme in itself, with obedience to the Law as man's chief obligation. The writings of Paul both focused on the ineffectual nature of the Law and the "new Israel" status of Jewish and gentile believers in Jesus, which also contributed to the widening rift as Christianity came to appeal more and more to gentiles.

Fourth, most importantly, perhaps, Christians became increasingly critical of the temple cult, as it came to be viewed as having been "built with human hands" (Acts 7:48). An indication is that the temple, from the Christian perspective, had become idolatrous in pre-70 CE Jerusalem, for the sacrifice of Jesus "once for all" had ended all need for further sacrifices. Christians themselves carried priestly offices of reconciliation. A "once for all" sacrifice through a single human being for the sins of the world did not set well with temple Pharisees who viewed the man Jesus as a threat to temple traditions.

Fifth, a further "rift" came when, as Roman legions began their journey towards Jerusalem under Titus to respond to the Jewish rebellion, passive Christians fled Jerusalem for the small town of Pella, leaving their countrymen to face the pending doom.

Sixth, the introduction of the *Birkat ha-Minim* prejudiced non-Christian Jews against Jesus of Nazareth. A Christology that affirmed the "oneness" of Jesus with Yahweh was an important factor that led to a negative response at Yavneh toward Jesus. Jesus had clearly stated his absolute "oneness" with the Father (John 10:30), and his many "I Am" statements in the Gospels were interpreted in light of the Holy Scriptures that spoke of the Holy One as "I AM." The Pharisees and temple leaders of Jesus' day clearly understood the connection that Jesus was making. Paul repeatedly referred to Jesus as "Lord" (*passim*). In Romans 1:3, 7, and in 5:1, and 11 Paul uses *passim* in the context of the Jewish hope for the coming of an anointed descendent of David who would restore Israel and through whom God's kingdom would be established forever. Many other factors would give rise to the final "parting" between the church and Judaism, but the *Birkat ha-Minim* provided a strong wedge that resulted in the final separation.

Seventh, in my view, the available historical data strongly suggests that the sages at Yavneh could not possibly conceal Jesus from the Jewish masses, *per se'*, for historical information about Jesus was both written and widely circulated from many perspectives, and tens of thousands of Jews were coming to faith in him. In addition, the sages understood that their positions as credible leaders were at best tenuous. The ordinary Jew viewed the sages with suspicion for they did not prevent the temple's destruction—*God had destroyed His own temple*, and unrecorded numbers of priests and Pharisees, along with the general Jewish population, had been slain without mercy.

The widening rift between the new Nazarene movement and its parent faith, Judaism, was more apparent after the destruction of Jerusalem. Still, early "seeds of division" were clearly apparent in the Gospel accounts with many confrontations between temple leaders and Jesus. The parents of the blind man in John's account, for example, were afraid of the actions of the Pharisees in the event that their son should confess that Jesus was the Messiah. "His parents...were afraid of the Jews (leaders); for the Jews had already agreed, that if any one should confess Him to be the Messiah, he should be put out of the synagogue" (9:22).

However, the New Testament examples of Christians being excluded from synagogues appear *incidental* and not widely practiced. It appears that a broader persecution and exclusion from the synagogue would happen later in the first quarter of the second century.

There has always been a dilemma when attempting to date the material in the Mishnah and Talmud. As documented above, dating textual material in the Yavnean period is nearly "guesswork". We do not know for certain when the condemnation of the "heretical writings" took place; it is not certain that the "heretics" described are really a wide range of groups that included Gnostics and Ebionites, or if Christians were specifically targeted. The evidence appears to lean to the former, which would date the events late in the Yavnean period under Gamaliel II (ca. 135 CE).

Further, caution must be taken in that many first century "Judaisms" competed with historic Judaism for equal status. Many false "messiahs" had arisen during a time when messianic expectations were nearly fever pitch, born out of Jewish apocalyptic writings that were unrelated to the Torah in particular, or the *tenach* in general. In many ways these false "messiahs" caused great concern among the sages which lead them to conclude that the real Messiah could not be in their midst, the true Messiah would not be self-deluded and "lead Israel astray," as Jesus is portrayed in the Talmud. On the contrary, to objectively consider a Messiah who "emptied himself" of all Self to redeem and lead Israel back to their Heavenly Father, and one who was the Visitation of God himself, was beyond both the theology and vision of the sages in the context of Roman domination.

Always in the shadows stood the cold and cruel hand of the Roman captor, tormentors and idolaters who hated both Israel's God and the Christian's Lord, whose pagan messiah was a mere Caesar who demanded the bended knee to blind worship. The very notion of this was odious to both Jews and Christians.

In this chaotic and confusing world arose Yohanan ben Zakkai, strong-willed and tenacious, but a lover of peace, Torah study, and faith in the one true Lord. With this historical context in view, Yohanan cautioned his disciples, "If you hear that the messiah has come, do not be quick to leave your field and run out to meet him." Apocalyptic idealism had no place in Yohanan's thinking or pragmatism; his single calling and task was to gather disciples from the ruins of the temple and fashion a new temple in the human heart through Torah study and prayer. Similarly, the new Nazarene movement that followed the calamity of the second temple destruction would teach their followers that believers in Jesus were, in reality, "temples of the Holy Spirit."

Rabban Yohanan ben Zakkai, visionary and noble leader, contemplated the meaning of two temple disasters in the history of his people Israel, and at Yavneh inscribed the prophet's creed in the hearts of his disciples: "I delight in loyalty rather than sacrifice, and in the knowledge of God rather than burnt offerings."

+ + +

In the second century CE, Roman Emperor Marcus Aurelius observed of Socrates that he used to call *popular beliefs* "monsters under the bed" — that "their true use is to frighten children." Popular beliefs often become urban legends that take root as historical fact, but when the light of truth is turned their way, the monsters take flight.

Historically, barriers to communication between Jews and Christians have existed that have muddied the waters of shared values and truth. To cast an early Jewish sage as a popular boogeyman who cast a spell over an entire nation is beyond the pale of reason. That a single, tenuous leader, could have succeeded in hiding Jesus is patently without historical evidence. That rabbis succeeded in hiding Jesus through the ages from all Jews again lacks historical evidence.

Did early rabbis influence their people? Most certainly, and with cause, especially in light of many false winds of doctrine and troublemakers who came along. Add to this the Imperial Roman Caesar who demanded worship and held the present and future of every living Jew in their sway. Superlative and vitriolic language by a minority of Evangelical popular writers is both inappropriate and not helpful in any dialogue.

Christians must seek to better understand the historical barriers that have divided Judaism and Christianity; popular myth and legend must be replaced with serious, objective research in order to compete in the ideological arena. Sadly, doing serious homework apart from enthusiasm remains a low priority on the list for some Evangelicals. Thus, a message for Christians would be to take up the intellectual pursuit of the truth. As Aurelius penned so eloquently eighteen centuries ago, "the truth never harmed anyone."

Likewise, a message to Jewish truth-seekers is perhaps best expressed by Jewish philosopher Martin Buber who, in the middle of the last century, exhorted Jews everywhere to "overcome their superstitious horror of Christianity...and to place it where it belongs in the spiritual history of Judaism."

Source Notes

Chapter One

1 Jacob Neusner, *The Body of Faith: Israel and the Church* (Valley Forge: Trinity Press International, 1996), 24.

2 Cf. Isaiah 52; 53; Jeremiah 31:31-34.

3 Cf. Luke 4:21; John 5:39; Mark 4:4; 7:8; Matthew 15:3.

4 Cf. Mark 2:21; 7:8; 1 Corinthians 11:2.

5 Cf. Matthew 6:4, 9; 7:21; 26:29; Mark 8:38; Luke 2:49; 11:2; 23:34; John 1:14; 8:18; 10:30; 14:2; 16:23; 20:17.

6 Cf. Mark 14:53-58. For a complete discussion of the trial and Crucifixion from the Christian perspective, see N.T. Wright, *Jesus and the Victory of God,* Part III: "The Reasons for Jesus Crucifixion," (Minneapolis: Fortress Press, 1996), 547-552. For the Jewish perspective, see Hugo Mantel, *Studies in the History of the Sanhedrin* (Cambridge: Harvard University Press, 1961), 254-302. Mantel's earlier argument is an expansion of his dissertation in which he propounds that "the "crime" which Jesus was supposed to have "plotted against the Temple" was one unknown in Judaism" (273). However, Wright directly confronts Mantel's argument and notes the following in reference to Mishna *Sanhedrin* 43a (also 107b): " The apparent oddity of Jesus being stoned and hanged is explained...the corpse must be hung on a gibbet, but taken down again before sunset in obedience to Deuteronomy 21:23. The notion of a forty-day appeal for defense is normally discounted"(548).

7 Cf. Mark 14:59-62; 15:1-2; John 18:29-38. Also, Wright, op. cit., 543-547.

8 Cf. Matthew 24:15-28, 42, 44; 25:13, esp. v. 34: "I tell you the truth, This generation will certainly not pass away until all these things

have happened." On Matthew 24:34, Robert L. Reymond comments: "This 'time text' places beyond all legitimate question the propriety of the preceding interpretation of Matthew 24:4-33, however strained it may have appeared at times to the modern reader, particularly in 24:29-31. His disciples had asked him about the 'when' of the destruction of the temple to which he had referred in 24:2, and he responded to their query by declaring that it would occur during that generation (see Matt 23:36 for additional confirmation of this fact), to be preceded by the 'sign' of Rome's army — the 'abomination that causes desolation" — surrounding Jerusalem" (cf., Robert L. Reymond, *A New Systematic Theology of the Christian Faith* (Nashville: Thomas Nelson, Publishers, 1998), 1005.

9 Historian Philip Schaff is here quoted at length on the edict of Claudius:

"The first historic trace of Christianity in Rome we have in a notice of the heathen historian Suetonius, confirmed by Luke (cf. Acts 18:1-2), that Claudius, about 52 AD, banished the Jews from Rome because of their insurrectionary disposition and commotion under the instigation of 'Crestus' (misspelled for 'Christus'). This commotion in all probability refers to messianic controversies between Jews and Christians who were not yet clearly distinguished at that time. The preaching of Christ, the true King of Israel, would naturally produce a great commotion among the Jews, as it did at Antioch, in Pisidia, in Lystra, Thessalonica, and Berea; and the ignorant heathen magistrates would as naturally infer that Christ was a political pretender and aspirant to an earthly throne. The Jews who rejected the true Messiah looked all the more eagerly for an imaginary Messiah that would break the yoke of Rome and restore the theocracy of David in Jerusalem.

"Their carnal millennarianism affected even some Christians, and Paul found it necessary to warn them against rebellion and revolution. Among those expelled by the edict of Claudius were Aquilla and Priscilla, the hospitable friends of Paul, who were probably converted before they met him in Corinth. The Jews, however, soon returned, and the Jewish Christians also, but both under a cloud of suspicion. To this fact Tacitus may refer when he says that the Christian superstition which had been suppressed for a time (by the edict of Claudius) broke out again (under Nero, who ascended the throne in 54)." Cf. Philip Schaff, *A History of the Christian Church*, vol. 1 (Philadelphia: RBDH Publishing, 1976), 172.

10 *Ioudaismos* (Judaism) occurs only in Galatians 1:13-14, and appears to describe the Jewish way of life as a whole having distinctions from other religions (cf. Ignatius *Phld*, 6:1 juxtaposed to Christianity, *christianismos*). The term originally connoted "to live like a Jew according to Jewish customs." The question debated among the early Jewish believers in Acts 15 was, in effect, "Could a Gentile be considered a part of the people of God if they did not conform to the requirements of the Law?" See Shaye D. Cohen, *The Beginnings of Jewishness* (Berkeley: University of California Press, 1999), 175-197. Cohen discusses the colloquial developments of *Ioudaizein* among Christians in early cultural developments

11 Michael L. Brown, *Our Hands Are Stained with Blood* (Shippenburg, PA: Destiny Publishing, 1992), 27ff.

12 Josephus, *Jewish War*, bk. 5, chap. 12, paragraph 3; chap. 13, paragraph 13.

13 Jacob Neusner, *A Life of Yohanan Ben Zakkai* (Leiden: Brill, 1970), 196-8. Hereafter: *Life*.

14 Ibid., 199.

15 Hal Lindsey, "From Abraham to the Middle East Crisis" Video Series (Palos Verdes, CA: Hal Lindsey Ministries).

16. Cf. Neusner interview, 8/26/99.

17 Grayzel, *A History of the Jews* (Philadelphia: the Jewish Publication Society, 1947), 194-195.

18 Ibid.

19 Brown, op. cit. Chapter Eight: "The Inquisition Isn't Over." For a full discussion of the denial of personal and civil rights of Jews by Christian authorities see Louis Goldberg: *Our Jewish Friends* (Chicago: Moody Press, 1977).

20 Note: Corrie ten Boom and Oskar Schindler are only a few. Orthodox Jewish rabbi Daniel Lapin, in his book, *America's Real War*, provides an alternative understanding of Jewish persecution through the ages by various groups, the church in general, and radical socialist movements in particular. Lapin is quoted at length in order to see the context of his argument: "To this day, Orthodox Jews still mourn the loss of our Holy Temple and the closeness to God that it made possible. Jews continued to incur tragedies, including the destruction of the second temple by the Romans in the year AD 70, the expulsion

of the Jews from Spain in 1492 and from England in 1290, and the numerous occasions when Jews were given the choice of converting to other religions or dying... There has been no shortage of tragedies to commemorate in Jewish history. If a Jew can still bring tears to his eyes when he thinks of an ancestor killed in medieval times, it is no surprise that he still has an instinctive reaction toward the medieval church, which was often the instigator of, or at least an accomplice to, the violence. But although the Holocaust is difficult to discuss dispassionately, I still think it is time for a reassessment.

"I do, however, want to make three points clear. First, although most parts of medieval Europe were certainly governed by religiously empowered authorities, the populations, particularly those elements that regularly delighted in pogroms, were mostly wild mobs. Let us remember a key difference between modern America and medieval Europe. In Europe, a politically and economically powerful clergy ruled largely illiterate mobs. In America, a powerless clergy presides over deeply religious, sophisticated, and educated Christians. In Europe there were centuries of pogroms; such as never been the case in America.

"Let's face up to another fact. Life in America has accustomed us to peace among various religious groups. In contrast, European religious life has been unpleasant for many people over the centuries. While, as a Jew, I mourn for my own people, historically Christian denominations in Europe tended to also persecute each other. If we are relying on European memories as our guide, not only Jews, but also Catholics, Baptists, Lutherans, and other groups have reason to distrust one another... As to the Holocaust itself, we need to concede...although Jews and Christians correctly see in the rise of Nazism a failure on the part of the church, Hitler was made possible by the triumph of scientific naturalism in Europe, not by organized religion. Nazism was, after all, 'Nationalized Socialism,' and any form of socialism has intellectual roots in the secular Left, not the religious Right.

"While centuries of anti-Semitism by the church certainly made Hitler's task a little easier, we also must recognize that in Lutheran countries such as Denmark, Finland, Norway, and Sweden, devout Christians, and often the church leadership itself, turned the rescuing of Jews into a religious mission. That fact cannot just be dismissed as irrelevant. Many Catholic and Protestant church leaders in Europe realized that Hitler hated God and the church. Many lost their lives. Only a society in which the church had already been weakened could breed Nazism. This is one of the reasons that I insist Jews should do everything in their power to support and encourage American Christians in their task of taking back the culture." Cf. Sisters, OR: Multnomah Publishers, 1999, 326, 327).

21 Cf. "Christianity Today," April 5, 1999, 23.

22 Ibid. op. cit., September 6, 1999, 24.

23 Phillip N. Moore, *Messiah Conspiracy: The End of History* (Atlanta: Conspiracy, Inc., 1996), 364.

24 *Ibid.*, 308-309.

25 Cf. Neusner interview.

26 Moore, op. cit., 308.

27 Ibid.

28 Hal Lindsey, op. cit.

29 *Life,* 182-183.

30 Gedaliah Alon, *The Jews in Their Land in the Talmudic Age* (Cambridge: Harvard, 1980), 289.

31 See discussion on this point in Chapter Four.

Chapter Three

1 Marc Block, *The Historian's Craft.* New York: Vantage Press, 1952, 50.

2 Ibid., 52. In its original Greek root, the word "history" means *research*, and implies the act of *judging the evidences* in order to separate fact from fiction. The opening line of Herodotus is sometimes translated not "these are the histories of Herodotus of Halicarnassus," but "these are the researches…" The word "research" can mean any sort of inquiry — into what is the case and into what has happened in the past. "Historical research" may be redundant and may be excused on the basis that it is necessary to distinguish between two kinds of inquiry or research — scientific and historical. Herodotus — the "father of history" — is credited for originating a style of writing that differed from poetry and story telling. He attempts to win the reader's af-

firmation not by the credibility of his narrative, but by providing the reader with some sources of information and the reliability of the documentary evidence upon which his narrative is based. Where the poet tells a likely story, the historian attempts to make credible statements about particular past events, to weigh the evidence himself, or as with this dissertation, to submit conflicting testimony to the reader who must render a verdict (cf. *The Great Ideas*. Mortimer J. Adler, Ed. [New York: Scribners, 1952], 307).

3 Ibid., 53. "In our language the term *History*," Hegel observes, "unites the objective with the subjective side...It comprehends not less what has happened than the narration of what has happened."

4 the two meanings we must regard as of a higher order than mere outward accident; we must suppose historical narratives to have appeared contemporaneously with historical deeds and events" (cf. Adler, op. cit., 307). Herbert Butterfield, "Moral Judgments in Philosophy," Meyerhoff, ed., 244.

5 Roger Kimball, "In Defense of Facts," *National Review*, Vol. LI, No. October 25, 1999, 45.

6 Ibid.

7 Simon Greenleaf, *The Testimony of the Evangelists* (Grand Rapids: Baker Book House, 1984), 7.

8 Ibid. op. cit., 9.

9 Kimball, op., cit., 45. [Emphasis added]

10 N.T. Wright: *Jesus and the Victory of God* (Minneapolis: Fortress Press, 1996), 542.

11 Ibid., 543.

Chapter Four

1 For one of the most complete discussions of early pilgrimage by Jews to the temple, see S. Safrai, *Pilgrimage at the Time of the Second Temple* (Tel Aviv, 1965).

2 Jacob Neusner, *A Life of Yohanan Ben Zakkai* (Leiden: E. J. Brill, 1970), 7.

3 See Ben Zion Wacholder, "Biblical Chronology in the Hellenistic World Chronicles," *HTR 61*, 1968, 451-81.

4 *Life*, 8.

5 Historical sources that pertain to the temple in Jerusalem are extensive. Saffria's *Pilgrimage*, cf. 123-234, remains the most extensive in detail, as does Alice Muehsam's, *Coin and Temple. A Study of the Architectural Representation on Ancient Jewish Coins* (Leeds, 1966). In addition, Edersheim's, *The Temple, Its Ministry and Services as They Were at the Time of Jesus Christ* (London, 1959), offers further detail in ritual, festivals, etc.

6 *Life*, 10.

7 Ibid.

8 Matthew 23:37.

9 Matthew 24:2; cf. also 19-21. Cf. Also Luke 21:6. Jacob Neusner, *Judaism in the Beginning of Christianity* (Philadelphia: Fortress Press, 1984), 19-20.

10 *Eusebius, Ecclesiastical History*, 3.5.2f. Eusebius cites Josephus as pertaining to the Christians heeding the word of the Lord some time before the Roman siege of Jerusalem, and escaping to the Galilean town of Pella. It appears that shortly after James' death that the church could no longer live in safety with its neighbors. Koenig believes the move was completed by 66, "though some believers may have remained behind in Judea and Jerusalem" (*Jews and Christians in Dialogue*, 64). No early church historian indicates that Christians took one side or the other, or that they suffered atrocities. It appears probable—based upon early Jewish sources—that Christians took a pacifist position towards the Roman war.

11 Cited by Neusner in *Life*, 11.

12 Solomon Grayzel, *A History of the Jews* ((Philadelphia: the Jewish Publication Society of America), 176. H.H. Ben-Sasson, ed.: *A History of the Jewish People* (Cambridge: Harvard University Press, 1976), 314-318.

13 Grayzel, 176-77.

14 Psalm 137:5-6 NASB.

15 Grayzel, 177.

16 Ibid., 177-8. Judean males in the diaspora before 70 CE were to pay taxes towards temple sacrifices at the rate of two drachmas or two denarii (1/2 shekel) per year which were kept in the temple treasuries

(4 Macc 4:3). In addition, other temple materials were stored there (m. 'Arak. 6:2-5). Belo (1981) and Goodman (1982) both provide substantial historical evidence that in the Herodian period priests and landowners gained control over peasants through loans, thus controlling land by means of debt defaults, and directing enormous agricultural products to their advantage. The heavy and competing taxation systems guaranteed that debts would escalate.

17 Cf. discussion by F.F. Bruce, *Israel and the Nations: The History of Israel from the Exodus to the Fall of the Second Temple* (Downers Grove: InterVarsity Press), 220-21.

18 *Life*, 11.

19 Ibid., 12. Hansen and Oakman contend that the powerful aristocracy, particularly the high priests and important priestly families, controlled the temple and were primary beneficiaries of it" (*Palestine in the Time of Jesus*, 146). Herod appointed high priests during the time of Jesus to control the temple. Mariamme the Hasmonean and Miriamme the daughter of Boethus, two of Herod the Great's wives, were both of priestly families, marriages that were designed to increase Herod's status and power (Jos. *Ant.* 18:93-95). The peasants perceived the temple system during the days of Herod as both oppressive and thievery, a sentiment argued by Jesus (Mark 11:17). Malina (1988:10) and Evans (1989) both argue that Jesus wanted to go beyond mere cleansing of the temple to the point of advocating its destruction. Though Jesus respected and assumed the relevance of temple involvement (Matthew 5:25) and respected some covenant institutions (Mark 1:44; Luke 17:4), he did view it as "a cave of bandits" and rebuked temple scribes for taking advantage of the poor (Mark 12:40).

20 Ibid., 12.

21 Genesis 6:9

22 Ezra 2:9; Nehemiah 7:14.

23 Cf. F. Brown, S.R. Driver, C.A. Briggs, Hebrew-English Lexicon of the Old Testament (Oxford, 1955); M. Jastrow, *Dictionary of the Talmud Babli* (New York, 1950). On R. Zakkai, cf. y. Yev. 8:3.

24 Matthew 2:7-8. In this passage we see the paranoia of Herod who carefully concealed his motives from the Magi. Herod had told the Sanhedrin why he was concerned about the Messiah, and "learned

from them carefully" (*ekribosen*), "learned exactly" or "accurately." It appears that Herod wanted to match the appearance of the star to the Magi with the Hebrew prophecies concerning Messiah. Verse 8 is more revealing with the use of the aorist participle, for they were to "search out accurately" concerning the Messiah child. That Herod wanted to receive word in order to worship him appears to be manipulative and devious.

25 E. Schurer, *A History of the Jewish People in the Time of Jesus Christ* (Edinburgh, 1890, 5 vols., hereafter: Schurer), Division I, vols. 1 and 2.

26 Cf. G. Alon, "On the History of the High Priesthood at the End of the Second Commonwealth" (Tel Aviv, *Ta. XIII*, 1941), 1-24.

27 Grayzel, 193.

28 Ibid.

29 Ibid., 194.

30 Ibid.

31 F. Grant, *Economic Background of the Gospels* (London, 1926), 105ff; Neusner, *Judaism*, 22-23.

32 Ber. R., 100:24; *Midrash Tannaim*, ed. D. Hoffman (Berlin, 1909), 226, 1.30; b. R.H. 31b; Sanhedrin 42:a.

33 Qoh. R.6:1, q.v.

34 Cf. M. Avi-Yohah, "Trade and Industry in the Land of Israel in the Roman-Byzantine Period," in B. Maisler, *et al*, Mishar, *Ta'asiah, ve'Omanut be' Erez yisra'el* [*Commerce, Industry, and Crafts in the Land of Israel*] (Jerusalem, 1937), pp. 85ff. For a discussion of the extent of Greek language usage in urban centers during the first century, see James H. Charlesworth and Loren L. Johns (ed.), *Hillel and Jesus: Comparative Studies of Two Major Religious Leaders* (Minneapolis: Fortress Press, 1997), 227-229. Hereafter: *Hillel and Jesus*.

35 Cf. Deut 6:6; Ex 20.

36 *Life*, 18-19.

37 Finkelstein, *Pharisees*, I, 1-43; see chart on pages 4-5.

38 For a study on the ordinary people of the land of first century Palestine, see A. Buchler, *The Galilean 'Am Ha' Arez* (Jerusalem, 1964),

trans. By I. Eldad of *Der galilasche Am-Ha' Ares des zweiten jabrhunderts*.

39 Shaye J.D. Cohen, *From the Maccabees to the Mishnah* (Philadelphia: Westminister Press, 1987), 225.

40 *Life*, 20-22.

41 *Manual of Discipline* 5.1. For a discussion of the various sects, see Josephus, *Antiquities*, Books XIII and XVIII; War II, pp. 119-66; Pliny, *Natural History*, V. 17, 73; and Philo, *That Every Good Man Is Free*, XII. Max Weber, *Ancient Judaism* (New York: the Free Press, 1952), 410-412.

42 Avot 1.5.

43 *Antiquities* 18.1.3. See also, *Hillel and Jesus*, 21ff.

44. *Life*, 23. Cf. Schurer, Second Division, vol. II, 10-28.

45 Ibid., 24. Cf. also George Foote Moore, *Judaism* (Cambridge, 1954, 3 vols.), I, 68-70. For a discussion of the Sadducees, see Jakob Jocz, *The Jewish People and Jesus Christ* (London: SPCK, 1949), 15-17; *Hillel and Jesus*, 205-210.

46 George Foote Moore, *Judaism In the First Centuries of the Christian Era: The Age of Tannaim* (Peabody: Hendrickson Publishers, 1960), I, 68-70. Cf. Neusner, *Judaism*, 25-28.

47 J. Juster, *Les Juifs dans l'empire romain* (Paris, 1914); Salo W. Baron, *A Social and Religious History of the Jews*, I-II, *Ancient Times* (Philadelphia, 1952); Alon, 196-205.

48 The most detailed analysis of the Sanhedrin of the first century is Hugo Mantel's, *Studies in the History of the Sanhedrin*(Cambridge, 1962). Mantel's work is an expansion of his dissertation. Cf. Alon, op. cit., 196-205.

49 See Mantel's discussion, op. cit., 268-275 in which he argues that the Sanhedrin of that era could not have imposed the death penalty on Jesus for blasphemy, breaking the Sabbath, or for threatening the destruction of the temple.

50 *Life*, 27. Cf. Alon, 207.

51 When Jerusalem fell to the Romans in 70 CE, followed by the ensuing massive migration of Jewish peasants and leaders to Yavneh, it became necessary for R. Yohanan ben Zakkai and the Beth Din to

reformulate the Jewish calendar as part of the overall public enactments.

52 *Life*, 27.

53 For an excellent discussion of Roman ethics and philosophy as they related to the Jewish worldview, see Edward Gibbon, *The History of the Decline and Fall of the Roman Empire* (London: Folio, 1984), vol. 1.

54 Avot 2.9.

55 Moore, I, 263, 416.

56 B. Shab. 15a.

57 *Life*, 34. Mantel provides a thorough discussion on the autonomous position of Yohanan in the first century Jewish Beth Din, see pp. 28-35 in *Studies in the History of the Sanhedrin*.

58 Cf. b. Shab. 14b, 15a, 17a, 19a, 30b, 31a; Bez. 16a, 20a; Hag 16a; Yoma 77b; Syuk 28a-b; Yev. 15a; Git 57a; Qid 43a; Nid 2a-b, 3a-b, 4a-b, 15a; y. Ma'aser Sheni 2.2, 2.3, *et al.*

59 Avot 1.15.

60 *Life*, 35-36.

61 *Ibid.*

62 Avot 1.12.

63 Avot 1.13.

64 Avot 1.14

65 Mishnah Shev. 10.3; 'Arakh. 9.4.

66 G. Alon, *A History of the Jewish People* (Cambridge: Harvard University Press, 1976), p. 319. After Cestius Gallus failed to take Jerusalem by force, resulting in his flight and retirement, the Beth Din leadership, among whom were prominent Sadducees, attempted to control Jewish affairs and made Ananus and Joseph ben Gorion governors of the city. They also appointed military commanders for numerous districts to prepare for the pending conflict. All efforts proved futile, factions committed horrible atrocities, and Jerusalem fell in 70 CE. As the Jews destroyed themselves from within the Romans watched from a distance, Rabban Yohanan ben Zakkai was smuggled out of the city in a coffin to General Vespasian's camp. A lengthy discussion

between the two resulted in a resettlement of Jews and their rabbis in the town of Yavneh (Roman: Jamnia).

There are three historical versions of Yohanan's escape, (Cf. Lam. R. on Lam. 1,5; Abot de-R. Nathan c.4; Gittin 56 a-b; see Neusner's discussion: *Life*, 155-166). Ben-Sasson argues that "Rabban Yohanan was initially a prisoner and was taken against his will to Yavneh, which, along with other towns, such as Ashdod and Gophna, served as a place of detention for those who had surrendered to the Romans" (320).

Scholars affirm that various towns served as detention centers for Jews, but the historian can only infer from the three accounts that Yohanan was forced against his will to settle at Yavneh. There is no historical evidence one way or the other; suffice it to say whether by force or compromise, Yohanan desired to start an Academy at Yavneh and the new emperor Vespasian granted his request. Alon argues that in the spring of 68 CE, when Vespasian began his siege of Jerusalem inclines him to reject the standard account of the general "giving: Yavneh to the Rabban and his disciples. The Tradition (Mishnah) is not clear with regard to any scenario. Alon suggests that because the Romans used various towns such as Ashkelon and Gaza as towns of retention for refugees following the war, it is likely that Yavneh was one such detention center, where Yohanan received permission only "to instruct his disciples," and where his personal entourage was permitted to practice their religion and engage in Torah study (cf., 97-98).

Alon observes that the conversations reported in Bekhiah 5a between Rabban Yohanan and the commander Controcos do not adequately demonstrate that Yohanan had special status or privilege with Vespasian. "At best," notes Alon, "they indicate the absence of government interference. Besides, these encounters are probably legendary" (Ibid, 98).

67 *Aboth Derabbi Nathan* B, 31.

68 Ibid.

69 G. Alon, *Jews in the Land*, op. cit., 86.

70 Moore, vol. I, 84.

71 Ibid., 85.

72 Cf. Mark 14:53, 55. See also Matthew 26:57, 59; Acts 4:5ff; 5:27, 34, 41; 6:12.

73 Ibid. p. 85.

74 See Neusner's, *A Life of Yohanan ben Zakkai*, as cited above. Other references by Neusner may be found in the bibliography.

75 L. Ginzberg, 'Bet Din,' *Jewish Encyclopedia*, II, 114ff. According to the tradition, the result of the dominant outcome of the Hillelites is recorded in as a legend: A voice from heaven was heard at Yavneh saying, "The teachings of both schools (Shammai and Hillel) are words of the living God, but in practice the halakah of the school of Hillel is to be followed" (cf. Jer. Berakot 3b; 'Erubin 13b).

76 Neusner, *Life*, 200-203. Cf. also Hans Conzelmann, *Gentiles, Jews, and Christians: Polemics and Apologetics in the Greco-Roman Era* (M. Eugene boring, Trans. Minneapolis: Fortress Press, 1992), p. 37.

77 Ibid. 37, 38; See also S. Simon, *Verus Israel: A Study of the Relations Between Christians and Jews in the Roman Empire* (135-425), Oxford: Oxford University Press, 1986.

78 Cf., Schurer, I, 556; See also *Sibylline Oracles* as an example.

79 Conzelmann, 38.

80 *Life*, 196.

81 Ibid.

82 "Nasi" was the term to designate the President of the Sanhedrin. The Tradition (Talmud) speaks of the Nasi as a learned judge—a Pharisee (See Hagigah, Mishnah 2:2 for a reference to the five sets of *zugot*, or "pairs" of the Sages: "The first of these held the office of Nasi, while the second in each case was Av Bet-Din—Presiding Justice."

83 Cf., Alon, *The Jews in Their Land*, op. cit., 101ff.

84 Cf. Alon's discussion on pp. 100-109.

85 Sheq. I:4; Eduy. 8:3.

86 Alon, 103.

87 Babra Batra. 10b.

88 See list by Alon, 103.

89 *Life*, 196.

90 J. Goldin, "The Period of the Talmud," in L. Finkelstein, ed., *The Jews, Their History, Culture and Religion,* I, 147. Neusner, *Life,* 196, cites also by comparison, G. Cohen, "The Talmudic Age," 160-1; cf. also, H. Graetz, *History,* II, 333, and Javitz, *Toledot,* VI, 1 f.

91 *Life,* 197. See G. Allon, "the Presidency of Rabban Yohanan ben Zakkai at Yavneh," Mehqarim, I, 254-273.

92 Schurer, History, I, ii, 191-206.

93 Cf. Milik, Ten Years of Discovery, 94-97.

94 See B.Z Bokser, *Pharisaic Judaism in the Transition,* 1-6. Bokser's analysis is admittedly conjectural concerning the fate of the others groups following the war.

95 *Life,* 198.

96 Ibid.

97 L. Finkelstein, *Pharisees and Men of the Great Assembly* (New York: 1950), 38. See also, Alon, op. cit., 93. Alon comments, "The (Pharisee) peace party, from the very start rejected the possibility of victory, and therefore made no effort at all to wrest freedom from the Romans. This grouping included some whom even before the outbreak of war had had no faith in the ability of their countrymen to manage an independent state worthy of the name. Looking around them, they saw internecine violence, bloodshed, and civil disorder verging on anarchy, especially after the death of Agrippa the First when the Sicarri and their ilk came to the fore. Nor were the established institutions of the society, especially the High Priesthood and its hangers-on, calculated to inspire much confidence."

98 Alon, 108.

99 Ibid., 108.

100 Mishnah Sotah 5:2.

101 Mishnah Yerushalmi Sanhedrin 1:18a.

102 Alon, 109.

103 See Professor Chayes' "Revue des 'etudes Juives," as quoted in Alon, 109.

104 Psalm 137: 1-6 (NASB).

105 Rabban Gamaliel II would later introduce new ordinances of Temple service.

106 Mishnah Rosh Hashanah 30a.

107 See the *baraitha* as quoted by the Talmud in Yerushalmi Sheqalim 8:51b.

108 Alon, 254.

109 Neusner, *Life*, 210-211.

110 The real point of debate is whether the *birkat-ha minim* malediction was pronounced during the time of Rabban Yohanan ben Zakkai, or later during the leadership of Rabban Gamaliel II. I believe that the *birkat-ha minim* is not the sole issue, but only a logical outcome of what the sages already believed about Jesus, regardless of when the pronouncement was initiated. At issue is the nature and scope of the Talmudic testimony concerning Jesus, which will be addressed following a discussion of the known historical activities of Yohanan ben Zakkai.

111 *Life*, 211. See also Allon, *Toledot*, I, 65-71.

112 See also Leviticus 8:21; Mishnah Sotah 40a.

113 The ceremonial act of purification by washing is a repeated them in the Old Testament, particularly in the psalms and prophets (Ps 26:6; 51:2; Is 1:16; in the same context, see also Heb 6:2; 9:10 and 10:22 for ritualistic washings that do not remove sin). On many occasions in the Gospels, Jesus dealt with the Pharisees over the emphasis of ceremonial washing juxtaposed to the washing of the inner heart (Matt 6:17ff; 15:2ff; Lk 11:38). Then again, repeated in the New Covenant was the spiritual "washing" away of sins through the blood of the atonement through faith in Jesus (Acts 22:16; 1 Cor 6:11; 1 Tim 5:10).

114 The term "halakhah" is used in the dissertation, and is found replete in Jewish literature. The term in Hebrew means "the way," or in a general sense, "law," and in Jewish literature tends to be associated primarily with Pharisaic and rabbinic Judaism. However, other groups in the Second Commonwealth also coined the term, such as found in the Dead Sea Scrolls, including Jubilees, all of which contains large amounts of prescriptive legal information, and texts that imply the observance of a form of "halakhah." For a detailed exposition, the reader is referred to *The Dictionary of Judaism in the Biblical Period* (Jacob Neusner, ed.), 268-270.

115 *Life*, 211.

116 *Lulav* refers to palm branch that was bound with myrtle and wil-

low, associated with the Feast of Sukkot (Tabernacles), represented as a major motif in Jewish art

117 Alon, Toledot, I, 68.

118 *Life*, 211.

119 Ibid.

120 Ibid., 214.

121 Ibid.

122 George Foote Moore: *Judaism*, vol. I, 87 [Italics added].

123 Alon, 275.

124 Ibid. 276.

125 Ibid.

126 Alon cites five passages in the Talmud to suggest that the meaning of *"gilyonim"* does not mean 'Gospels" but rather "sheet" of writing materials, such as a parchment sewn to others in order to make a scroll. On the issue of anti-Semitism and the New Testament, see Claudia J. Setzer, *Jewish Responses to Early Christians: History and Polemics*, 30 − 150 CE), Minneapolis: Fortress Press, 1994.

127 Tos. Yadaim 2:13; Bavli Shabbat 116a; Yerushalmi. Ibid. 16:15c.

128 Tos. Shabbat 13 (12); Bavli and Yerushalmi, ibid.

129 Shabbat 116b. Alon suggests that there is a play on words in the uncensored versions.

130 See Ginzberg in *JBL* 1922, 122, note 19, who admits the possibility that *euangelion* could be implied, but that there is no relationship to the Jewish attitude to these books. Only the *'azkarot'* are intended. In the context of the Talmud's use of the word *"aven gilyon"*, and cites Tos. Yadaim 2:11 as support.

131 *Jewish Studies in Memory of Israel Abrahams*. New York, 1927, 210. Note Herford's metaphor of Judaism and Christianity like two bodies in opposite orbits (213), but at Montefiore notes in *The Old Testament and After*, Judaism was drastically affected by the new Christian movement in the same way that the earth was affected by the appearance of the moon (164ff.).

132 Ibid. 211.

133 Ibid. 45.

134 Moore, *Judaism*, III, n. 110.

135 R. Travers Herford, *Christianity in Talmud and Midrash*, 200ff; also p. 122.

136 *Tractate Berakot*, 7a, from Cohen's Cambridge 1921 translation, as cited by Jocz, 46.

137 Jocz, *The Jewish People and Jesus Christ*, for which see the discussion on pp. 46-51.

138 The "minim" once addressed Rabban Gamaliel, "Whence do we know that the Holy One, blessed be He, will resurrect the dead?" He answered: "From the Torah, the Prophets and the Hagiographa" but they refused to accept his proofs (*Sanhedrin*, 90b). Herford suggests that this is not an instance where the Minim rejected the resurrection as a Scriptural doctrine, but only the warrant for the doctrine in the Holy Scriptures. Herford interprets them to be Christians who believed the resurrection "was subsequent on the resurrection of Christ" (cf. *Christianity in Talmud and Midrash*, 231ff).

139 John 9:22; 12:42-43; 16:2-3. In John 9:22 we see the most complete statement that "the Jews had already agreed that anyone who confessed Jesus to be the Messiah would be put out of the synagogue." Other scholars who link the *Birkat ha-Minim* to statements by John pertaining to the expulsion of Christians from the synagogue include Lindars, Schnackenburg, Townsend, and Barett. Davies views the curse as an anti-Christian measure, regardless of whether it is in the context of the Fourth Gospel or not (W.D. Davies, *The Setting of the Sermon on the Mount* [Cambridge: Cambridge University Press, 1966] 275-78).

140 Ibid.

141 The rabbinic reference here is attributed to Samuel the Small at Yavneh and implies that any person who fails in repeating it would be removed (b.Ber. 28b). Justin supplies a third piece of the puzzle, according to Martyn, who complains that Jews cursed Christ and Christians in the synagogue (cf. *Dialogue*, 16:4; 96:2; 137:2).

142 Claudia Setzer, *Jewish Responses to Early Christians: History and Polemics*, 30-150 CE (Minneapolis: Fortress Press, 1994), 89.

143 Setzer, 89.

144 R. Kimelman provides the most detailed response to the theory that *Birkat ha-Minim* applied to Christians specifically, in his "Birkat

Ha-Minim and the Lack of Evidence for an Anti-Christian Jewish Prayer in Late Antiquity," *Jewish and Christian Self-Definition* (vol. 2; ed. E.P. Sanders, *et al.*; Philadelphia: Fortress, 1981) 226-44. Scholars who do not affirm the broad use as an anti-Christian prayer include Cohen (*Maccabees*, 227); P. Schafer ("Die sogenannte Synode von Jabne," *Judaica* 31 [1975] 54-64, 116-24); and D. hare (*Jewish Persecution* [Cambridge: Cambridge University Press, 1967] 54. R. Whitacre, in his *Johannine Polemic* (SBL Dissertation Series 67; Chico: Scholars Press, 1980) provides a summary of the current debate.

145 J.D. Cohen, 227.

146 Ibid. 227-228.

147 Ibid. 228.

148 J. Mann, "Genizah Fragments of the Palestinian Order of Service", Hebrew Union College Annual 2 (19250, 269ff.

149 Dunn, 7.

150 Justin, *Dialogue* xvi, xcvi.

151 Dunn, Ibid.

152 Ibid. for which see discussion on pp. 7-10. B. Pixner comments: "The only expression of Judaism to survive was the Pharisaic brand. In Yavneh (Jamnia) the followers of the Pharisaic *halakhah* gathered under the leadership of Yohanan Ben-Zakkai and reorganized the Sanhedrin. They felt the strong rivalry that came from the Judeo-Christian movement. What until then had been a tolerated expression of Judaism, so that these Messianic Jews continued to partake in the synagogue service, now had to be cut off radically. This was done by adding to the *shemoneh esreh* prayer the *birkat ha-minim* with special mention of the *Nozrim*. Even though modern studies suggest that this Decree of Yavneh was not applied radically in all locations, it was doubtless the decisive event excluding the messianic Jews from worshipping the rabbinic synagogues (James H. Charlesworth, ed. *Hillel and Jesus*, 212. Sigal holds to the view that the *nozrim* were Christians and that the *minim* designation was a broad term to encompass miscellaneous sectarians, possibly Gnostics. Sigal observes that Gamaliel II had long since deposed Yohanan ben Zakkai, "a man of compromise," that by the time of Gamaliel II, Christians were seen as an encumbrance and hindrance. Thus, to acknowledge Jesus as Messiah was to decline faith in a future Davidic restoration as per the twelfth

and fourteenth benedictions. Sigal comments: "Judaic tempers had not yet cooled since 70, and were heating up again for the action that culminated in the Bar Kokhba rebellion in 132. Thus in his confrontation with Pilate Jesus says Pilate calls him a king whereas his function is to witness the truth. In this way, and in several others, John redefines the messianic concept moving from the traditional Jewish expectation to a new Christian definition" (Phillip Sigal, *The Emergence of Contemporary Judaism: Part One: From the Origins to the Separation of Christianity*. Pittsburgh: Pickwick Press, 1980, 429, 430.

153 Ibid., 10.

154 Jacob Neusner, ed. *The Encyclopedia of Judaism* (New York: Continuum, 1999), vol. 3, 1139.

155 Moore, "Canon," 122ff.

156 Wilson, 177

157 Justin stated that Trypho had read a Gospel and participated in an argument in refutation of his own teachers (*Dialogue* 10:2-3; 38:1; 112:4).

158 Wilson, 178.

159 Cf. Jacob Neusner, ed. *The Encyclopedia of Judaism,* vol. 3, 1139.

160 Neusner, *Encyclopedia*, vol. 3, 1135.

161. Ibid.

162 Ibid. for which see full discussion on pp. 1135-1139; also, Wilson, pp. 178-183. Dunn argues elsewhere that simply because Christianity was another Judaism, it was not "heresy" as such, that even during the time of the Second Commonwealth, "even the most virulent never accused the members of other groups of having left the Jewish community. Quoting Schiffman, Dunn observes that ""Sinners they were, but Jews all the same." In fact, Jewish status could never be cancelled, even for the most heinous offences against Jewish law and doctrine.

163 Tos. Hul. II:24. See also Bavli, Av. Zar. 16:b-17a. The Talmud provides many more details, As Alon observes, the "bit of minut" which Rabbi Eliezer had enjoyed was something that Jacob of Sikhnim the healer had personally learned from Jesus himself. It has been suggested that this very Jacob may have been James the son of Alphaeus,

or James the Lesser mentioned in Mark 2:18; 15:40 (See Alon, *The Jews in the Land*, 293ff).

164 Alon, 293.

165 Cf. Klausner, 35, 38, 42-46.

166 Klausner, *Jesus*, 18f.

167 Heinrich Liable, *Jesus Christus in Talmud*. Berlin, 1891, 88.

168 Jocz, 58.

169 Klausner, 19.

170 Wilson, 185.

171 B. Sanhedrin. 43a.

172 b. Sabb. 107b.

173 b. Sabb. 104b. Most scholars believe that the original ben Stada was a Jewish heretic accused of witchcraft and sorcery, calling forth his incantations from Egyptian magical arts.

174 Wilson, 185.

175 Rabbinic literature contains no information concerning the life of John, whose activity was important enough to be mentioned by Josephus (Cf. *Ant.*, XVIII, v, 2.

176 Jocz, 58.

177 Danby, 37; Jocz, 58.

178 Jocz, 59.

179 *Yeb*. Iv, 13: Danby's translation; this is R. Joshua's definition of a bastard: (The offspring of any union) for which the participants are liable for death at the discretion of the court.

180 Jocz, 59.

181 Note Klausner's note on Hebrew source material, op. cit., 18.

182 Jocz, 59.

183 Ibid. Jocz, though an older work, provides the most complete list of scholars and their works to date, cf. 425-435, for which see. The legendary source titled the *Tol'dot Jesu* is viewed by the overwhelming majority of scholars to be a fifth century CE writing. Hugh Schonfield's argument is clearly presented by Jocz 960-62) along with a rebuttal by Jocz, for which see, Ibid. The Talmudic tradition is pre-

sented in detail as most scholars agree that it originated in the aged of Tannaim, and is particularly Yavnean.

184 *M. Jeb.* Iv, 13, cp. *Bab. Shab.* 104b.

185 *Bab. Shab.* Ibid. Note that "*Miriam megaddeliah nashaia*" is a play on "*Miriam Magdalaah*", i.e. Mary Magdelene. See Klausner, 22f.

186 *Bab. Sanh.* 107b.

187 This accusation is found early in the ministry of Jesus, cf., Matt 10:25; 12:24, 27; Mk 3:22; Lk 11:15, 18, 19. Justin in his *Dialogue* also hints of it (c. 69). See Wilson's discussion of the accusation of sorcery and magic, 185-193.

188 *Bab. Sanh.* 107b.

189 Ibid.

180 Ibid. 103a.

191 Jer. Taan. 65a; Jesus is not mentioned by name, Herford notes, but there is no doubt that He is meant.

192 *Bab. Sanh.* 106a.

193 *Tos. Sanh.* X. 11; *Jerus. Sanh.* 25c, d.

194 *Tos. Sanh* IX, 7; *Bab. Sanh.* 43a.

195 *Bab. Sanh* 106b; *Bab. Gitt.* 56b, 57a.

196 *Bab. Sanh.* 43a; *M. Sanh.* X, 2. See Herford's discussion in R. T. Herford, "Christianity in Jewish Literature", in *Hastings Dictionary of Christ and the Gospels*, II, 877ff, as cited by Jocz, 337.

197 Jocz observes that the names of the disciples are given as Mattai (Matthew), Naqai (Luke), Nezer (pun on *Nozrim*), Buni (Nicodemus or John), and Todah (Thaddeus). For further discussion see Klausner, 19.

198 Edgar Hennecke, *Handbuch zu den neutestamentlichen Apokryphen.* Tubingen, 1914, 71. Italics added by Hennecke.

199 Wilson, *Related Strangers*, 193.

200 Ibid.

201 Ibid.

202 *Life*, 10-12. Cf. Wilson, 193.

203 1 Kings 5:5.

204 Isaiah 64:11 NASB.

205 Cf. Wacholder, "Biblical Chronology in the Hellenistic World Chronicles," *HTR 61*, 1968, 451-81.

206 *Life*, 8.

207 *Life*, 8. Cf. Saffria, Pilgrimage, cf. 123-234; Alice Muehsam, *Coin and Temple: A Study of the Architectural Representation on Ancient Jewish Coins*; Edersheim, *The Temple, Its Ministry and Services as They Were at the Time of Jesus Christ* . Cf. *Life*, 10.

208 Matthew 23:37. Matthew 24:2; cf. also 19-21. Cf. Also Luke 21:6. Cf. Neusner, *Judaism in the Beginning of Christianity*, 19-20.

209 *Life*, 11

210 Cf. Bruce, *Israel and the Nations: The History of Israel from the Exodus to the Fall of the Second Temple*, 220-21.

211 Cf. Mishnah Lam. R. on Lam. 1,5; Abot de-R. Nathan c.4; Gittin 56, a-b.

212 Cf. Neusner, ed., *The Encyclopedia of Judaism*, vol. 2, 874-888, see for detailed discussion on "Messiah". Neusner observes, "Indeed, two commonplaces of Western history are that, in first century Palestine, enhanced Jewish anticipation of the messiah's arrival was the backdrop for the emergence of Christianity and that conflicting opinions about the messiah's appearance, identity, activity, and implications caused the division between Judaism and Christianity." (874). Again, "The figure of the messiah emerges from the loss of the Davidic dynasty and of Israel's political autonomy" (875).

213 *Life*, 20-22.

214 Cf. Luke 19:2, 5, and 8. Neusner's discussion in *Life*, pp. 53-56.

215 G. Alon, *Jews in the Land*, 86.

216 Many opposed Yohanan at Yavneh, such as the Men of Bathyra. Sadducee priests who survived the destruction probably avoided Yohanan's academy. They gathered at Lud where they formed their own academy, and afterward, many were associated with Gamaliel II (Cf. Neusner, *Life*, 215.

217 Cf. Conzelmann, *Gentiles, Jews, and Christians: Polemics and Apologetics in the Greco-Roman Era*, 37. S. Simon, *Verus Israel: A Study of the Relations Between Christians and Jews in the Roman Empire* (135-425).

218 Cf., Schurer, I, 556.

219 "Nasi" designated "president" of the Beth Din. The Talmud refers to the Nasi as a learned judge — a Pharisee (Cf. Hagidah, Mishnah 2:2. See also, Alon, *The Jews in Their Land*, 101ff.

220 Cf. Chayes, "Revue des 'etudes Juives," as quoted in Alon, 109.

221 Psalm 137: 1-6 (NASB). Rabban Gamaliel II would later introduce new ordinances of Temple service. Cf. Mishnah Rosh Hashanah 30a. See the *baraitha* as quoted by the Talmud in Yerushalmi Sheqalim 8:51b.

222 Neusner, *Life*, 210-211.

223 Ibid., 211.

224 Ibid., 211.

225 Neusner, *Encyclopedia*, vol. 3, 1135.

226 Mishnah Rosh Hashanah 2:8-9

227 Dunn, *Jews and Christians*, 20.

228 Cf. James h. Charlesworth, ed. *The Messiah: Developments in Earliest Judaism and Christianity* (Minneapolis: Fortress Press, 1992), 281ff.

229 Antiquities, trans. William Whiston (Hendrickson Publishers, 1987), 531.

230 Ibid.

231 Leo Rosten, *The Joys of Yiddish* (New York: Pocket Books, 1968), 478.

232 *War*, 2:444-448.

233 *The Jewish Encyclopedia*, vol. X (New York: Funk & Wagnalls, 1912), 252.

234 Cf. Neusner, ed., *The Encyclopedia of Judaism*, vol. 2, 874-888.

235 Alon, *The Jews in the Land*, 298.

236 Justin Martyr (Dialogue XL), *Contra Celsum* VIII:61.

237 *Recognitiones* II 45, and *Homilia* II 40, as cited by Alon, Jews in the Land, 300.

238 Alon, 300, 301.

239 It is an interesting aside that many messianic congregational

leaders will exhort their congregations to face east when reciting the *Shema* during worship.

240 Alon, 305.

241 Dunn, 19.

242 Ibid., 2023.

243 Bruce Chilton and Jacob Neusner, *Judaism in the New Testament: Practices and Beliefs* (London: Routledge, 1995), 5.

244 Ibid.

245 Cf., Setzer, *Jewish Responses to Early Christians*, 89.

246 Ibid. R. Kimelman argues against the theory that *Birkat ha-Minim* was broadly applied to Christians in, "Birkat Ha-Minim and the Lack of Evidence for an Anti-Christian Jewish Prayer in Late Antiquity," *Jewish and Christian Self-Definition* (vol. 2; ed. E. P. Sanders et al.; Philadelphia: Fortress, 1981) 226-244. Other scholars also doubt the wide usage of the term as an anti-Christian "prayer" (Cohen, *Maccabees*, 227; D. Hare, Jewish Persecution [Cambridge: Cambridge University Press, 1967] 54, *et al.*

247 b.Ber. 28b.

248 Setzer, 89.

249 *Dial.* 16.4; 47.4; 96:2; 137.2.

250 John 5:39, 45-47; 8:12; 10:34-39.

251 Jocz, 57.

252 Emil Schwaab, *Historische Einfuhrung in das Achtzehngebet.* (Beitrage zur Forderung christl. Theologie, herausg. A. Schlatter u. W. Lutgert, heft V, 1913, as cited by Jocz.

253 Danby, *The Jew and Christianity*, London, 1927, 11-13.

Selected Bibliography

Primary Works

Eusebius. *Ecclesiastical History*. Translated by C.F. Cruse. Peabody, MA: Hendrickson Publishers, 1998.

Holy Scriptures. Revised by Alexander Harkavy. New York: Hebrew Publishing Company, 1951.

Josephus—Complete and Unabridged. Translated by Paul L. Maier. Grand Rapids: Kregal, 1988

Philo. Translated by C.D. Yonge. Peabody, MA: Hendrickson Publishers, 1993.

Mishna: Oral Teachings of Judaism. Translated by Eugene J. Lipman. New York: W.W. Norton & Company, 1970.

Mishna: A New Translation. Translated by Jacob Neusner. London: Yale University Press, 1988.

New Testament Background: Writings from Ancient Greece and the Roman Empire That Illuminate Christian Origins. Edited by C.K. Barrett. San Francisco: Harper-Collins, 1987.

Nicene and Post-Nicene Fathers. Volume 1: Eusebius: Church History, Life of Constantine the Great, and Oration in Praise of Constantine. Philip Schaff, Editor. Peabody, MA: Hendrickson Publishers, Inc., 1995.

Readings In the Classical Historians. Edited by Michael Grant. New York: Charles Scribners Sons, 1992.

Secondary Works
Books

Anderson, J.N.D. Christianity: *The Witness of History*. London: Tyndale, 1969.

128

Baron, Salo W. *A Social and Religious History of the Jews*, I-II, Ancient Times (Philadelphia, 1952).

Aurelius, Marcus. *Meditations*. Gregory Hays, trans. New York: The Modern Library, 2002.

Barrett, C. K. *The Gospel of John and Judaism*. London: SPCK, 1975.

Belo, Fernando. *A Materialist Reading of the Gospel of Mark*. Trans. Matthew J. O'Connell. Maryknoll: N.Y.: Orbis, 1981.

Ben-Sasson, H.H. ed. *A History of the Jewish People*. Cambridge: Harvard University Press, 1976.

Bloch, Marc. *The Historian's Craft*. New York: Vantage Books, 1953.

Bright, John. *A History of Israel*. Philadelphia: Westminster Press, 1981.

Brown, Colin. *Christianity $ Western Thought: From the Ancient World to the Age of Enlightenment*. Vol. 1. Downders Grove: InterVarsity Press, 1990.

Brown, Michael L. *Our Hands are Stained with Blood*. Shippensburg, PA: Destiny Image Publishers, Inc., 1997.

Brown, R. E. *The Gospel According to John* (I-XXI), 2 vols. AB. Garden City: Doubleday, 1966-70.

Bruce, F.F. *Jesus and Christian Origins Outside the New Testament*. Grand Rapids: Eerdmans, 1974.

_____. *The New Testament Documents, Are They Reliable?* Downers Grove: Inter-Varsity Press, 1972.

Bruce F.F. *Israel and the Nations: The History of Israel from the Exodus to the Fall of the Second Temple*. Downers Grove: InterVarsity Press.

Buber, Martin. *On Judaism*. Edited by Naham N. Glatzer. New York: Schocken Books, 1967.

Callan, T. *Forgetting the Root: The Emergence of Christianity from Judaism*. New York: Paulist, 1986.

Cameron, Averil. *The Later Roman Empire: AD 284 – 430*. Cambridge: Harvard University Press, 1993.

Carroll, Ken. *The Fourth Gospel and the Exclusion of Christians*.

Chandler, Walter M. *The Trial of Jesus From a Lawyer's Standpoint*.

Charlesworth, ed., *Jews and Christians: Exploring the Past, Present and Future.* New York: Crossroad, 1990.

Collingwood, R.G. *The Idea of History.* Oxford: Oxford University Press, 1994.

Conzelmann, Hans. *Gentiles, Jews and Christians: Polemics and Apologetics in the Greco-Roman Era.* Minneapolis: Fortress Press, 1992.

Crawford, Michael. *The Roman Republic.* Cambridge: Harvard University Press, 1992.

Cohen, Abraham. *Everyman's Talmud: The Major Teachings of the Rabbinic Sages.* Forward by Jacob Neusner. New York: Schocken Books, 1949.

Cohen, Shaye J.D. *From the Maccabees to the Mishna.* Philadelphia: Westminster Press, 1989.

_____. *The Beginnings of Jewishness: Boundaries, Varieties, Uncertainties.* Berkeley: University of California Press, 1999.

Dictionary of Judaism in the Biblical Period: 450 BCE. To 600 CE. Peabody: Hendrickson Publishers, Inc., 1996.

Dimont, Max I. *Jews, God and History.* New York: Mentor Books, 1964.

Dray, William H. *Philosophy of History* (Second Edition). Englewood Cliffs: Prentice Hall, 1993.

Durant, Will. *The Story of Civilization* (Part III: "Caesar and Christ). New York: Simon and Schuster, 1944.

Dunn, J.D.G. *The Parting of the Ways.* London: SCM; Philadelphia: Trinity Press International, 1991.

_____. *Jews and Christians: The Partings of the Ways AD 70-135.* WUNT 66; Tubingen J.C.B. Mohr/Siebeckm 1992.

Edersheim, Alfred. *Sketches of Jewish Social Life.* Peabody, MA: Hendrickson Publishing Company, 1994.

_____. *The Life and Times of Jesus the Messiah.* Philadelphia: McDonald Publishing Co., 1976.

Encyclopedia Judaica. "Anti-Semitism". Jerusalem: Keter Publishing House Ltd., 1974.

_____. "Zionism." Jerusalem: Keter Publishing House Ltd., 1973.

Engerg-Pedersen, Troels. *Paul in His Hellenistic Context*. Minneapolis: Fortress Press, 1995.

Evans, C.A. and Hagner, D.A. *Anti-Semitism and Early Christianity: Issues of Polemic and Faith*. Minneapolis: Fortress, 1993.

Freudmann, Lillian C. *Anti-Semitism in the New Testament*. New York: University Press of America, 1994.

Freyne, Sean. Galilee, *Jesus and the Gospels: Literary Approached and Historical Investigations*. Philadelphia: Fortress Press, 1988.

Gager, J. G. *The Origins of Anti-Semitism: Attitudes Toward Judaism in Pagan and Christian Antiquity*. New York: Oxford University Press, 1985.

Gibbon, Edward. *The History of the Decline and Fall of the Roman Empire*. 8 vols. London: The Folio Society, 1997.

Gillespie, Thomas W. *The First Theologians*. Grand Rapids: William B. Eerdmans Publishing Company, 1994.

Goldberg, Louis. *Our Jewish Friends*. Chicago: Moody Press, 1977.

Goldman, Hersh. *History of the Jewish People: The Second Temple Era*. Mesorah Publications, 1982.

Gordon, Cyrus H., and Rendsburg, Gary A. *The Bible and the Ancient Near East*. New York: W.W. Norton & Company, 1997.

Grabbe, Lester L. *An Introduction to First Century Judaism: Jewish Religion and History in the Second Temple Period*. Edinburgh: T&T Clark, 1996.

Graetz, H. *History of the Jews*. Jewish Publication Society, 1893.

Grant F. *Economic Background of the Gospels*. London: 1926.

Grant, Robert M. *Constantine: The Rise and Triumph of Christianity in the Roman World*. New York: Harper & Row, 1990.

Grant, Michael. *History of Rome*. New York: History Book Club Publication, 1978.

_____. *Nero*. London: The Folio Society, 1998.

Grayzel, Solomon. *A History of the Jews From the Babylonian Exile to the end of World War II*. Philadelphia: The Jewish Publication Society of America, 1947.

Green, W.S. ed. *Persons and Institutions in Early Rabbinic Judaism*. BJS 3. Atlanta: Scholars Press, 1977.

Greenleaf, Simon. *The Testimony of the Evangelists: Examined By the Rules of Evidence Administered in Courts of Justice*. Grand Rapids: Baker Book House, 1984.

Gurary, Noson. *Chasidism: Its Development, Theology, and Practice*. Jerusalem: Jason Aronson Inc., 1997.

Habermas, Gary R. *The Historical Jesus: Ancient Evidence for the Life of Christ*. Joplin, MO: College Press Publishing Company, 1997.

Hanson, K.C., and Oakman, Douglas E. *Palestine in the Time of Jesus: Social Structures and Social Conflicts*. Minneapolis: Fortress Press, 1998.

Hare, Douglas. *The Theme of Jewish Persecution of Christians in the Gospel According to St. Matthew*. Cambridge: Cambridge University Press, 1967.

Harvey, Van A. *The Historian and the Believer*. Chicago: University of Illinois Press, 1966.

Hatch, Edwin. *The Influence of Greek Ideas and Usages Upon the Christian Church*. Peabody, MA: Hendrickson Publishers, 1995.

Hayes, John H., and Mandell, Sara R. *The Jewish People in Classical Antiquity*. Louisville: Westminster John Knox Press, 1998.

Heinemann, J. *Prayer in the Talmud*. Berlin: de Gruyter, 1977.

Hellenistic Commentary to the New Testament. Edited by M. Eugene Boring, Klaus Berger and Carsten Colpe. Nashville: Abingdon Press, 1995.

Henry, Carl F.H. *The Identity of Jesus of Nazareth*. Nashville: Broadman Press, 1992.

Hengel, Martin. *Studies in Early Christology*. Edinburgh EH2 2LQ: T & T Clark Ltd., 1995.

Hillel and Jesus: *Comparative Studies of Two Major Religious Leaders*. Edited by James H. Charlesworth and Loren L. Johns. Minneapolis: Fortress press, 1997.

Jocz, J. *The Jewish People and Jesus Christ: A Study in the Relationship Between the Jewish People and Jesus Christ*. London: SPCK, 1949.

Judaism. Edited by Arthur Hertzberg. New York: George Braziller, 1962.

Judaisms and Their Messiahs at the Turn of the Christian Era. Edited by Jacob Neusner, William Scott Green and Ernest S. Frerichs. Cambridge: Cambridge University Press, 1987.

Juster, Dan. *Jewish Roots: A Foundation of Biblical Theology.* Shippensburg: Destiny Image Publishers, 1995.

Kac, Arthur. *The Missiahship of Jesus.* Minneapolis; Fortress, 1975.

Kaplan, Mordecai M. *Judaism as A Civilization.* New York: Thomas Yoseloff, 1934.

Kimelman, R. "*Birkat Ha-Minim* and the Lack of Evidence for an Anti-Christian Jewish Prayer in Late Antiquity." *Jewish and Christian Self-Definition*, vol. 2. Ed E.P. Sanders, A. Baumgarten, and A. Mendelson, 226-244. Philadelphia: Fortress Press, 1980-82, 2:226-244, 391-403.

Koenig, John. *Jews and Christians in Dialogue.* Philadelphia: Westminster, 1979.

Kung, Hans. *Judaism: Between yesterday and Tomorrow.* New York: Crossroad Publishing Company, 1991.

Kysar, R. *The Fourth Evangelist and His Gospel: An Examination of Contemporary Scholarship.* Minneapolis: Augsburg, 1975.

De Lange, N. *Origen and the Jews: Studies in Jewish-Christian Relations in Third-Century Palestine.* Cambridge: Cambridge University Press, 1976.

Laible, Heinrich. *Jesus Christus in Talmud.* Berlin, 1891.

Lapin, Daniel R. *America's Real War.* Sisters, OR: Mulnomah Publishers, 1999.

Lightfoot, John. *A Commentary on the New Testament from the Talmud and Hebraica.* 5 vols. Peabody, MA: Hendrickson Publishers, 1997.

Lindars, B. "The Persecution of Christians in John 15:18 — 16:4a." In *Suffering and Martyrdom in the New Testament.* Ed. W. Hornbury and B. McNeil, 48-69. Cambridge: Cambridge University Press, 1981.

Lindsey, Hal. "From Abraham to the Middle East Crisis." (Video

Series). Hal Lindsey Ministries, P.O. Box 4000, Palos Verdes, CA 90274.

Ludemann, g. *Opposition to Paul in Jewish Christianity*. Philadelphia: Fortress, 1989.

Mantel, Hugo. *Studies in the History of the Sanhedrin*. Cambridge: Harvard University Press, 1961.

Martyn, J. L. *History and Theology in the Fourth Gospel*, Second Edition. Nashville: Abingdon Press, 1979.

Meeks, W. "Am I a Jew?—Johannine Christianity and Judaism." In *Christianity, Judaism and Other Greco-Roman Cults: Studies for Morton Smith at Sixty*, pt. 1. Ed. Jacob Neusner 163-86. Leiden: Brill, 1975.

Meier, Christian. *Caesar*. Translated from the German by David McLintock. San Francisco, Harper-Collins, 1982.

Montaigne, Michel de. *The Complete Essays of Montaigne*. Translated by Donald M. Frame. Stanford, CA: Stanford University Press, 1976.

Moore, George Foot. *Judaism in the First Centuries of the Christian Era: The Age of Tannaim*. 2 vols. Peabody, MA: Hendrickson Publishers, 1997.

Montgomery, John Warwick. *The Shape of the Past: A Christian Response to Secular Philosophies of History*. Minneapolis: Bethany Press, 1975.

Neusner, Jacob *et al.* *The Encyclopedia of Judaism* (3 vols.). New York: Continuum, 1999.

Neusner, Jacob and Chilton, Bruce D. *The Body of Faith: Israel and the Church*. Valley Forge: Trinity Press International, 1996.

Neusner, Jacob. *The Body of Faith: Israel and the Church*. Valley Forge: Trinity Press International, 1996.

_____. *Development of a Legend*. Leiden: E.J. Brill, 1969.

_____. *A Life of Yohanan Ben Zakkai: Ca. 1-80 CE*. Leiden: E.J. Brill, 1970.

_____. *Eliezer ben Hyrcanus*. 2 vols. Leiden: E.J. Brill, 1973.

_____. *From Politics to Piety: The Emergence of Pharisaic Judaism*. Englewood Cliffs, N.J.: Prentice-Hall, 1973.

_____. *First Century Judaism in Crisis: Yohanan Ben Zakkai and the Renaissance of Torah.* New York: Abingdon Press, 1975.

_____. *A History of the Mishnaic Law of Purities.* Vals. 1-22. SJLA 6. Leiden: E.J. Brill, 1974-77.

_____. *Judaism in the New Testament.* London: Routledge, Ltd., 1995.

_____. *Judaism in the Beginning of Christianity.* Philadelphia: Fortress Press, 1984.

_____. *Rabbinic Judaism: Structure and System.* Minneapolis: Fortress Press, 1995.

_____. *The Intellectual Foundations of Christian and Jewish Discourse.* London: Routledge, Ltd., 1997.

Overman, J. A. *Matthew's Gospel and Formative Judaism.* Minneapolis: Fortress, 1990.

Parks, James. *The Foundations of Judaism and Christianity.* London: Vallentine, Mitchell & Company Limited, 1960.

_____. *The Conflict of the Church and the Synagogue: A Study of the Origins of Anti-Semitism.* London: Soncino, 1934..

_____. *Judaism and Christianity.* Chicago: University of Chicago Press, 1948.

Pranaitus, Justin B. *The Talmud Unmasked: The Secret Rabbinical Teachings Concerning Christians.* New York: E.N. Sanctuary, 1939.

Sanders, E.P. *Who Was a Jew? Rabbinic and Halakhic Perspectives on the Jewish-Christian Schism.* Hoboken, NJ: Ktav, 1985.

Safrai, Shmuel. "The Temple": *The Jewish People in the First Century: Historical Geography, political History, Social, Cultural and Religious Life and Institutions. Compendia Rerum Iudaicarum ad Novum Testamentum,* vol. 2. S. Safrai and M. Stern, eds. Philadelphia: Fortress, 1976.

Schaff, Philip. *History of the Christian Church.* 8 volumes. Philadelphia: McDonald Publishing Company, 1976.

Schoeps, H.J. *Jewish Christianity: Factional Disputes in the Early Church.* Philadelphia: Fortress, 1969.

Schurer, Emil. *A History of the Jewish People in the Time of Jesus Christ.* 5 vols. Peabody, MA: Hendrickson Publishers1994.

Schussler, E. ed., *Aspects of Religious Propaganda in Judaism and Early Christianity. University of Notre Dame Center for the Study of Judaism and Christianity in Antiquity 2;* Notre Dame, IN: University of Notre Dame Press, 1976.

Segal, A.F. *Two Powers in Heaven: Early Rabbinic Reports About Christianity and Gnosticism.* SJLA 25; Leiden: E.J. Brill, 1977.

Setzer, Claudia. *Jewish Responses to Early Christins: History and Polemics, 30-150 CE.* Minneapolis: Fortress Press, 1994.

Sigal, Philip. *Judaism: The Evolution of Faith.* Eerdmans, 1988.

Simon, S. *Verus Israel: A Study of the Relations Between Christians and Jews in the Roman Empire – 135-425.* Oxford: Oxford University Press, 1986.

Smith, Morton. *Studies in the Cult of Yahweh.* Vol. 2. Edited by Shaye J.D. Cohen. Leiden: E.J. Brill, 1996.

Snell, Daniel C. *Life in the Ancient Near East: 3100-332 B.C.E.* New Haven: Yale University Press, 1997.

Staiman, Mordechai. *Waiting for the Messiah.* Jerusalem: Jason Aronson Inc., 1997.

Starr, Chester G. *A History of the Ancient World.* New York: Oxford University Press, 1991.

Stemberger, Gunter. *Jewish Contemporaries of Jesus: Pharisees, Sadducees, Essenes.* Translated by Allan W. Mahnke. Minneapolis: Fortress Press, 1995.

Steinsaltz, Adin. *The Essential Talmud.* Translated from the Hebrew by Chaya Galai. London: Jason Aronson Inc., 1976.

Steinberg, Milton. *Basic Judaism.* New York: Harcourt, Brace & World, Inc., 1947.

Stern, David H. *Jewish New Testament Commentary.* Clarksville: Jewish New Testament Publications, Inc., 1992.

Stone, Michael E. (ed.). *Jewish Writings of the Second Temple Period: Apocrypha, Pseudepigrapha, Qumran Sectarian Writings, Philo, Josephus.* Philadelphia: Fortress Press, 1984.

The Book of Acts in Its Ancient Literary Setting. 2 vols. Edited by Bruce W. Winter and Andrew D. Clarke. Grand Rapids: William Eerdmans Publishing Company/The Paternoster Press Carlisle, 1993.

The Oxford Classical Dictionary. (Third Edition). Edited by Simon Hornblower and Antony Spawforth. New York: Oxford University Press, 1996.

The Oxford Companion To Classical Civilization. Edited by Simon Hornblower and Antony Spawforth. New York: Oxford University Press, 1998.

Tillich, Paul. *A History of Christian Thought: From Judaic and Hellenistic Origins to Existentialism.* Edited by Carl E. Braaten. New York: Simon and Schuster, 1968.

Townsend, J. "The Gospel of John and the Jews: The Story of a Religious Divorce." In *Anti-Semitism and the Foundations of Christianity.* Ed. A. Davies, 72-97. New York: Paulist, 1979.

Troels, Engberg-Pedersen, ed. *Paul in His Hellenistic Context.* Minneapolis: Fortress Press, 1995.

Weber, Max. *Ancient Judaism.* Translated and Edited by Hans H. Gerth and Don Martindale. New York: The Free Press, 1952.

Wells, Colin. *The Roman Empire.* Cambridge: Harvard University Press, 1984.

Wilken, Robert L. *The Christians as the Romans Saw Them.* New Haven: Yale University Press, 1984.

Wilson, S.G., ed., *Anti-Judaism in Early Christianity,* vol. 2, "Separation and Polemic. Studies in Early Judaism and Christianity 2"; Waterloo, ON: Wilfrid Laurier University Press, 1986.

Wright, N.T. *The New Testament and the People of God.* Minneapolis: Fortress Press, 1992.

_____. *Jesus and the Victory of God.* Minneapolis: Fortress Press, 1996.

Articles

Brown, R.E. "The Problem of Historicity in John." CBQ 24 (1962) 1-14.

Cohen, S.J.D. "The Significance of Yavneh: Pharisees, Rabbis, and the End of Jewish Sectarianism." HUCA 55 (1984), 27-53.

Culpepper, R. A. "The Gospel of John and the Jews". RevExp 84 (1987) 273-288.

Finkelsten, Louis. "The Pharisees, Their Origin and Their Philosophy," HTR XXIII (1930), 185ff.

Gereboff, J. "Rabbi Tarfon," BJS 6. Atlanta: Scholars Press, 1979.

Goodman, Martin. "The First Jewish Revolt: Social Conflict and the Problem of Debt." JJS 33:417-27.

Green, W.S. "What's in a Name? The Problematic of Rabbinic Biography.'" Approaches to Ancient Judaism: Theory and Practice (1978) 1.77-96.

_____. "Context and Meaning in Rabbinic 'Biography.'" Approaches to Ancient Judaism (1980) 2.97-111.

Horbury, W. "The Benediction of the *Minim* and Early Jewish-Christian Controversy." JTS 33 (1982), 19-61.

Kanter, S. "Rabban Gamaliel II." BJS 8. Atlanta: Scholars Press, 1979.

Katz, S.T. "The Separation of Judaism and Christianity After 70 CE: A Reconsideration," JBL 103, 1984.

Martyn, J. L. "Glimpses into the History of the Johannine Community." In L'Evangile de jean. Ed. M. de Jonge, 149-175, Gembloux: Ducolot, 1977.

Neusner, Jacob. "The Formulation of Rabbinic Judaism: Yavneh (Jamnia) from AD 70 to 100." ANRW 2 (1979) 19.2.3-42.

Pancaro, S. "The Law in the Fourth Gospel." Supp. To NovTSup 42. Leiden: Brill, 1975.

Saldarini, A.J. "Johanan ben Zakkai's Escape from Jerusalem: Origin and Development of a Rabbinic Story." JSJ 6 (1975) 189-204.

Smith, D. M. "The Life Setting of the Gospel of John." RevExp 85 (1988), 433-444.

Zahavy, T. "The Traditions of Eleazar Ben Azariah." BJS 2. Atlanta: Scholars Press, 1977.

ISBN 1-41205689-6

9 781412 056892